PARTICIPATORY RURAL APPRAISAL TECHNIQUE FOR FARM WOMEN

PARTICIPATORY RURAL APPRAISAL TECHNIQUE FOR FARM WOMEN

By
Neelma Kunwar
*Deptt. of Extension
Communication Management
Faculty of Home Science
C.S. Azad University of
Agriculture & Technology
Kanpur (U.P.)*
&
Kirti Shukla

DISCOVERY PUBLISHING HOUSE PVT. LTD.
NEW DELHI-110 002

Published by:
Tilak Wasan

DISCOVERY PUBLISHING HOUSE PVT. LTD.
4831/24, Ansari Road, Prahlad Street
Darya Ganj, New Delhi-110002 (India)
Phone: +91-11-23279245, 43764432
Fax: +91-11-23253475
E-mail: parul.wasan@gmail.com
info@discoverypublishinggroup.com
web: www.discoverypublishinggroup.com

First Edition: 2011
ISBN: 978-81-8356-716-9

Participatory Rural Appraisal Technique for Farm Women
© 2011, **Authors**

All rights reserved. No part of this publication should be reproduced, stored in a retrieval system, or transmitted in any form or by any means: electronic, mechanical, photocopying, recording or otherwise, without the prior written permission of the author and the publisher.

> This book has been published in good faith that the material provided by authors is original. Every effort is made to ensure accuracy of material, but the publisher and printer will not be held responsible for any inadvertent error(s). In case of any dispute, all legal matters are to be settled under Delhi jurisdiction only.

Dedicated to

My constant source of inspiration
and encouragement
............my loving husband

Mahesh Shukla
with love, regards and gratitude

Preface

The widespread adoption of the rhetoric of participation in development is welcome for the legitimacy and space it accords to those who genuinely want to practice it. In parallel, the phenomenal spread of practices described as PRA has shown practical ways in which participation can be made real, and has inspired and provided opportunities for many. These successes have brought many benefits. Among the best have been the empowerment of poor people through their own analysis and action, and new insight gained by professionals into their realities and priorities.

PRA methods are an important part of such processes - their power and popularity have given rise to a great demand for manuals. The desire to know the right way to do something is deeply ingrained in us from our educational systems. If there are manuals for vehicle maintenance, cooking and flying an aeroplane why not for PRA method ? It is, after all, comforting to have a book of instructions and know that when you are uncertain you can go in to it and look up what to do next. Some have resisted this, for them, the key insight was embodied in the manual with a single sentence. Use your own best judgment at all times in which all the other pages were blank. The message was experience, experiment, invent and learn for yourself and then, "write your own manual". Any manual, it has been felt, would inhibit creativity, experimentation and growth'. This is then, a source of ideas and advice, not a set of marching orders.

There are many versions now of PRA, and interpretations of its principles and methods. The spirit of PRA is that each of us can decide and evolve these for ourselves. Each of us can think out our own changing watchwords for what the essence of good practice is. For me these include diversity, inventiveness, self-critical awareness and empowering process. It is especially with diversity that this book makes a significant contribution, by indicating and describing an astonishing range methods. Intelligently used as a source of ideas, it can also contribute to inventiveness by inspiring facilitators to be creative and to encourage the creativity of poor people, empowering them to appraise and analyse their lives and conditions. It can also point to the need and importance of yet other methods for planning and taking action part of the excitement of PRA is that there is no end. There will always be more to discover in our search for better ways of doing things. And we can be grateful for the way this book provides us with a resource of experience and insights on which to draw, helping us to travel further and faster on our individual paths of exploration.

The encouragement and suggestion that I have received from my teachers Dr. Bharti Singh & Dr. J.P. Singh, friend Mrs. Mitlash Verma and Komal Chandra any my daughter Km. Litasha Kunwar continues to be a source of inspiration for me.

I take this opportunity to acknowledge my dept of gratitude to the publisher Discover Publishing House Pvt. Delhi for their painstaly efforts.

Neelma Kunwar

Acknowledgement

My debts are great and too many which I can not even dare to acknowledge, especially of almighty God, who bestowed on me the courage to carry out this research work.

It is a golden opportunity and proud privilege to work under the most talented and inspiring guidance of *Dr. Neelma Kunwar* (D.Sc.) Associate Professor, Department of Extension and Communication Management (ECM), C.S. Azad University of Agriculture and Technology, Kanpur and Chairperson of my Advisory Committee. Her untiring supervision persistent, encouragement, unending zeal, conspicuous ability and constructive criticism have always been a constant source of my inspiration and achievements. I am extremely indebted to her for being meticulous throughout investigation and preparation of this manuscript.

I also express my heartfelt thanks and gratitude to *Dr. (Mrs.) Rekha Dayal,* Associate Professor, Department of Family Resource Management, College of Home Science, *Dr. R.N. Prasad,* Associate Professor (Statistics), Department of Agricultural, Economics and Statistics, *Dr. R.N. Verma,* Associate Professor, Department of Agronomy and *Dr. H.B. Dwivedi,* Head of Dairy Science, C.S. Azad University of Agriculture and Technology, Kanpur who are the members of my Advisory Committee, for their effluent efforts, timely guidance and creative suggestions during the tenure of the present study.

Words can never express the indebtedness but I dare to take this opportunity to pay my sincere appreciation to *Dr. Arun Kumar Srivastava,* Assistant Statistician, Department of

Crop Physiology and *Dr. D.K. Srivastava,* Programme Coordinator of 'Krishi Vigyan Kendra, Auriaya, for not only helping me but also took keen interest throughout the course of investigation. Had they not taken painstaking efforts and inspiring attitude, this research work would not have been accomplished.

I am equally express my veneration to *Dr. Irfan Beg,* SMS (Horticulture) *Dr. Vikas,* SMS (Animal Science), *Dr. Yogendra* SMS (Ext. Education) *Dr. Sandeep* SMS (Agronomy) and all Krishi Vigyan Kendra Staff of Auariya who cooperated me during my study period.

From the core of my heart, uncountable words of cordial veneration and gratitude are dedicated to pious feet of my grand mother *Smt. Surajmukhi Shukla,* father-in-law *Sri Ashok Shukla,* my mother in-law (Late) *Smt. Malti Shukla,* my father *Sri S.G. Dwivedi* and my mother *Smt. Manju Dwivedi* for their love, affection, good blessing, constant encouragement and inspiration, showered upon me for the achievements of my present assets. I also express my wormth appreciation to my brother *Mr. Rajeev Dwivedi,* my sister *Miss. Preeti,* Dipti and Tripti, my sister-in-law, *Mrs. Shrdha* and her husband *Mr. Raman Bajpai,* my brother in law *Mr. Anoop Shukla* and her wife *Mrs. Sweta Shukla.* I am also thankful to my younger brother-in-law *Mr. Ashish* and Sumit Bajpai who extended moral support and timely help and a constant inspiration to me during my research work.

From the very special of my heart, I would like to thanks to my caring and loving husband *Mr. Mahesh Shukla,* who had to bear the most loneliness during the entire period of the present investigation. All words and lexicon are not sufficient to express my reverence to him for his unfailing love, unfathomable constant recursion, support and encouragement throughout the time.

I am getting short of words to express my special regard to my *Sneha* aunty, *Manorama* aunti and *Mithlesh* aunty and all loving cousins who cooperated in my bad times and helped me to overcome my mental tiredness and distress. I am also grateful for the enormous affection, constant enocuragement, cordial support and best wishes extended by those whose presence one can feel always at the hour of need. Their love and moral support helped me to cope up with problems and showed me the path of success.

I offer my warmest thanks and indebtedness to my friends. Archana, Phoo di, Amita, Neha, Master Aditya, Shobhit, Shubham, Santosh and all others, for their constant love, help and encouragement.

I am also thankful to Mr. A.K.S. Sengar, Office Secretary, Office of the Registrar, C.S. Azad University Kanpur for neat and clean typing of this manuscript and Mr. Ajit for designing and graphics of the data besides other timely help.

Lastly, the cooperation provided by the entire staff at college of Home Science, C.S. Azad University of Agriculture and Technology and all the respondents of the Study area and greatly acknowledged.

Kirti Shukla

Contents

Preface

Acknowledgement

1. **Introduction** 1

   Strengths of PRA—PRA and Rapport Building—How Participatory is PRA?—Participatory Methods—Principles and Techniques—Women and Formal PRAs—Constraints Faced by Farm Women—Priortisation of Problems by Rural Women—Some Observations on Women's Problems—Objectives—Justification of the Study.

2. **Review of Literature** 16

3. **Profile of the Study Area** 33

   District Kanpur—Location—Area—Population—Sub-divisions Tahsils—Topography—River System and Water Resources—Rivers—Ganga—Yamuna—Lakes—Climate—Rainfall—Temperature—Humidity—Distribution between Urban and Rural Area.

4. **Research Methodology** 39

   (*i*) Locale of the Study—(*ii*) District under Study—(*iii*) Selection of Blocks—(*iv*) Villages Identified for the Study—(*v*) Selection of Respondents—B. Variables and their Operationalization—1. Independent Variables—2. Dependent Variables—Time of Investigation—Hypotheses—Statistical Measurement.

5. **Findings and Discussion** 50
    I. Socio-economic Status of Farm Women—Involvement of Farm Women in Agriculture Activity through PRA Technique Time Line—Involvement of Women in Household Activities through PRA Technique—Time—Contraints.

6. **Summary and Conclusion** 104
    Objectives—Research Methodology—Major Findings—Suggestions and Policy Implication.
    Bibliography 117
    Index 123

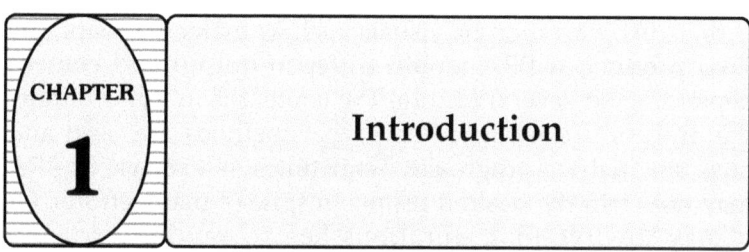

Introduction

Participatory Rural Appraisal (PRA) is a methodology for interacting with villagers, understanding them and learning from them. It involves a set of principles, a process of communication and a menu of methods for seeking villagers participation in putting forward their points of view about any issue and enabling them to do their own analysis with a view to make use of such learning. It initiates a participatory process and sustains it. Its principles and the menu of methods help in organizing participation.

PRA is a means of collecting different kinds of data, identifying and mobilizing intended groups and evoking their participation and also opening ways in which intended groups can participate in decision-making, project design, execution and monitoring. It provides an alternative framework for data collection and analysis. Because of its participatory nature, it is a useful methodology focus attention on people, their livelihoods and their inter-relationships with socio-economic and ecological factors.

PRA constitutes a process of involvement with rural people for indigenous knowledge building exercises. It is a way of learning from and with villagers to investigate, analyse and evaluate constraints and opportunities. It helps to make informed and timely decisions regarding development projects. The participation of rural people can be facilitated through PRA for planning, implementing and monitoring of rural development programmes.

PRA is a process of participation with the villagers in which rapport building paves the way for them to perform their own analysis and to express themselves whether by means of verbals like narration or visuals such as making a map. The final product of PRA would differ in output and content depending on several factors. The content is in terms of how the process is established and what methods are used and how the analysis progresses. Sometimes an exercise in PRA may not yield the desired results in spite of many efforts. Or it may involve long durations before anything fruitful happens. Hence, the output of PRA cannot be predicted with any degree of certainty. Sometimes more time is required and better efforts and newer ways can make things happen.

Participatory Rural Appraisal (PRA) is a further development of PRA. The mode of PRA has been mainly extractive "we" have gone to rural areas to learn and then left to analyze the data. To quote a recent source : "The major advantage of PRA is its ability to generate, in a short time, information that can then be used by development planners". In contrast, PRA shifts more of the presentation and analysis of information to "them", more of which is undertaken there in the field.

The term PRA was probably first used in Kenya to describe village-level investigations, analysis and planning undertaken by the National Environment Secretariat in association with Clark University, USA. A form of PRA was introduced in India in a joint exercise of the Aga Khan Rural Support Programme (AKRSP) in Gujarat and the International Institute for Environment and Development, London. Since then it has evolved rapidly and spread, with MYRADA, an NGO based in Bangalore taking a leading role, with other NGOs such as AKRSP in Ahmedabad, Action Aid in Bangalore, SPEECH in Madurai, Tamil Nadu and PRADAN and Krishi Gram Vigyan Kendra in Ranchi, Bihar, all active and innovating, Nepal also now has a PRA network with over 150 members.

PRA can be defined as a semi-structured process of learning from, with an by rural people about rural conditions.

It shares much with its parent, RRA, but is distinguished form it in practice in South Asia by correcting two common errors: roles of investigation are reversed; and rushing is replaced by relaxation and rapport.

1. The roles of teacher and learner are reversed. They teach us. Rural people own more of the process and output. Investigation, presentation and analysis are done more by the people themselves, including visual sharing of information in maps, models and diagrams and quantification is made and presented by them. Most of the activities that we thought necessary—interviewing, transects, mapping, measuring, analysis, planning—are done jointly with villagers or by them on their own. The appraisal and learning are not just by us from them, but with them and by them.

2. Rapport with villagers is primary. To achieve good rapport often requires the reorientation and relaxation of outsiders, and critical self-awareness. Rural people's suppressed incapacity and ignorance have often been an artifact of our ineptitude. With few exceptions, we—the outsider professional community—have not known how to help them to express, share and enhance their knowledge. The ignorance of rural people has been a self-sustaining myth, created and maintained by our confident and overweening clumsiness. By wagging the finger, holding the stick, sitting on the chair behind the table; by dominating and overwhelming thought and speech; by being rushed and impatient; by demanding information and answers; by believing that we know and they are ignorant, that they are the problem and we are the solution; by failing to sit down with respect and interest and listen and learn—in these ways we have impeded expression of knowledge and creative analysis by rural people.

The approach and methods of PRA recently brought together and developed tend to overcome these obstacles.

The keys is the outsiders should have appropriate attitudes, demeanor and behaviour. These include :
- participation by the outsider
- respect for rural people
- interest in what they know, say and show
- patience, wandering around, not rushing and not interrupting
- humility
- materials and methods which empower villagers to express, share, enhance and analyze their knowledge.

Given these, the results can be astonishing. I have a prejudice that rural people know more and are more rational and capable than most outsider professions give them credit for. But even so, IO have been amazed during the past year at the wealth of detailed information presented and analyzed. Social anthropologists and others can legitimately pointed out that much of this has been known and tried in the past. What is new is the combination of attitudes, behaviour and methods and their synergism.

Strengths of PRA

1. Visual sharing, diagrams, maps or quantification are presented physically by rural people in a manner they readily understand, since they have created it and that can be cross checked and amended. Successive approximation is thus built into the process.
2. Ranking and scoring, rather than measuring. Of course, measurements and estimates can be and are sought. But especially for sensitive information like income or wealth, people are often willing to present relative values when they would conceal or distort absolute values. In seasonal analysis, for example, people readily use seeds or other counters to show relative amounts of income and expenditure by month. Similarly, with changes and trends over time, relative values can be

given. Ranking items by people's own criteria, and scoring different items out of ten, five or three, have also proved feasible and popular.

3. Combinations and sequences of methods have proved powerful and practical. Participatory mapping and modelling, where villagers make their own map or model on the ground or on paper, leads easily and naturally to other activities, such as discussing routes for walking transects in which they are guides and to household listings and wealth ranking, to identifying numbers and types of people in a community and to marking in other details.

4. The approach and methods are popular and empowering. Questionnaires are often a bore for all concerned. PRA methods are often enjoyed. We have had to learn not to interview and not to interrupt when people are being creative with a map or model, when they are thinking, when they are reflecting on estimates. People are no longer "respondents". They are players, performers, presenters and own their play, performance and presentation. And the word "fun" comes into the development vocabulary.

Participatory Rural Appraisal (PRA) methods in India are increasingly taken up by public sector organizations as well as by NGOs among whom they have been pioneered. While PRA methods are successfully employed in a variety of project planning contexts—and with increasing sophistication—in other situations the practice of PRA faces constraints. In particular, it is suggested that as participatory exercises, PRAs' involve 'public' social events, which construct 'local knowledge' in ways, which are strongly influenced by existing social relationships. Information for planning is shaped by relations of power and gender, and by the investigators themselves; and that certain kinds of knowledge are often excluded. Social dominance and gender are not universally experienced as constraints in the practice of PRA. In this sense it is not a conclusion or a judgment, but an indication of the continuing need for context-specific methodological adaptation, especially as PRA is more widely employed in the public sector. PRA needs to be complemented by other methods of 'participation', which generate the changed awareness and new ways of knowing which are necessary to locally-controlled innovation and change.

The popularity of participatory rural appraisal (PRA) techniques in rural research and project planning comes in large part from their use in generating information at the community level directly with members of the community. Such information is held to be more reliable and more relevant to community interests than that generated by conventional social research methods (Chambers, 1983, Chambers, 1991). Improving both the quality of information available to planners and communication between outsiders and community members is central to the rationale for participatory approaches, at least for projects with a more instrumental notion of participation where PRA has made major in-roads. Many development efforts take place in highly complex social and physical environments, which places a premium on the use of people's knowledge and judgments (e.g. in assessing new technologies). Techniques of PRA not only draw on the complexity and sophistication of people's technical and social knowledge and their practical expertise in managing livelihoods (etc.), but also draw on hitherto unrecognized abilities of diagrammatic and symbolic representation among informants through a range of mapping and other techniques useable by non-literate peoples (c.f. PRA Notes, 1988-92). The effectiveness of location specific project strategies based upon local knowledge equally depends upon the quality of information feedback and learning, and for this PRA increasingly finds successful application in methods of project monitoring and evaluation.

PRA and Rapport Building

Rapport is itself a very difficult quality to identify. The term describes a relationship between outsiders and the community, and implies the trust, agreement and cooperation necessary for the pursuit of participatory approaches to development. However, this relationship is usually described from only one point of view—that of the outsider. Effective rapport in practice often represents the set of assumptions that outsiders have about the 'accessibility' of villagers and the likelihood of effective communication with them. In the case of the project in the absence of agreed criteria and indicators quite different assumptions were made by different people about what should be taken as signs of 'good rapport'. Some fieldworkers emphasized participation in village meetings at which the project objectives were explained others stressed the strength of links with and cooperation of local leaders others pointed to the number of household visits made. Several early problems in using PRA in fact related to mistaken assumptions and misread signs of 'rapport'. In practice, communication of the project's identify and gaining acceptance of its intended activities, as basis for undertaking PRAs, proved to be a complex process. It was, moreover, only possible through the processes of critical reflection on practice, which the project developed. The following paragraphs indicate the nature of the problem.

How Participatory is PRA?

The objectives of undertaking PRA are likely to vary with the stage of a work. In early stages of KRIBP there was a clear trade-off between the objectives of 'rapport-building' and 'information gathering'. Maximising opportunities for participation was not always compatible with getting the best, most systematic, or most accurate data. Local teams varied in their emphasis, but it was widely accepted that early PRAs should give priority to the quality of project-community relations over the quantity of information output. Ensuring adequate coverage and quality of data was a task pursued subsequently in an interactive fashion.

However, despite efforts to broaden contacts, PRAs are unlikely to be equally accessible or open to all sections of the community. Initial PRA activities of the project rarely involved a full cross section of the village community. Gender, age, education and kinship all influence participation in PRAs. In Rajasthan village, for example, one of the two major descent groups in the community initially took a leading role, and the other, although not excluded was less centrally involved. This highlights the risk that without further work the priorities and action plans identified for the village will reflect a narrow set of interests. Not only are some sections of a village under represented, but also some participation is discontinuous over the course of the PRA. Above all, participation by women has in all PRAs been both limited and discontinuous. The reasons for non-participation, encompassing both practical (e.g. time, distance) and social (e.g. social factions and alliances) factors. In some cases, strong leaders were able to 'mobile' wide group participation in others, individual factors of interest and curiosity appeared foremost. Without some means of recording and monitoring participation in PRAs, non-participation and the information distortions it causes is often unrecognized.

Firstly, as public and collective events, PRAs tend to emphasise the general over the particular (individual, even, situation etc.), tend towards the normative (what ought to be rather than what is) and towards a unitary view of interests, which underplays difference. In other words, it is the community's 'official view' of itself, which is projected. Communities are often most solidary when facing outsiders (Robertson, 1984). People may express their equality and unity of opinion to outsiders through generalized expressions "we think, we want etc.". These 'rhetorical expressions of integrity of the community' are not to be mistaken for the absence of distinct and perhaps conflicting interests (Cohen, 1989). The tendency to give normative information may be encouraged by faulty interviewing techniques (Mitchell and Slim, 1991), but often the very structure of the PRA sessions—group activities leading to plenary presentations—assumes and encourages the expression of consensus.

Participatory Methods—Principles and Techniques

Participatory methods for impact assessment are most commonly associated with the spread of diagramming and visual techniques which began to be developed in the 1970s. These originated in a number of scientific disciplines interested in analysis of complex systems; biological science, ecology, agricultural economics and geography. It became increasingly important to work with farmers to develop more sophisticated models to explain their responses to development programmes. The increasing influence of applied anthropology in development agencies form the 1980s also led to greater awareness of the need for a more sophisticated understanding of poverty, social processes and grassroots perspectives on development. By the end of the 1980s diagramming techniques bringing together the insights from these different disciplines had been combined into a flexible methodology commonly referred to as Rapid Rural Appraisal (RRA). Parallel to these developments in the South, methodologies like Soft Systems Analysis and Cognitive Mapping also became increasingly common in areas like management consultancy, organizational research and planning. Here diagrams were used for institutional analysis, highlighting problem areas and brainstorming possible solutions. Workshops for organizations and enterprises included senior executives and managers.

By the mid 1990s it was becoming increasingly evident that the mechanical application of these techniques was often failing to really reach and capture the views of poor people, particularly women, children and socially excluded. There was renewed interest in methodologies for participation drawing on earlier traditions of participatory action research which had been long established as an integral part of many grassroots organizations in the South. In India for example SEWA and other women's organizations based their programmes on the findings of focus group discussions in the 1970s and 1980s, MYRADA and AKRSP developed.

Women and formal PRAs

By far the most important observation from the first PRAs carried out as part of the KRIBP project was the minimal participation of women. Very few women attended these PRAs, their involvement was discontinuous and they did not play a role in the round-up and planning sessions with which the PRAs often concluded. This raises both specific questions about women's participation in the PRAs in the project, and more general issues concerning assumptions about the 'accessibility' of women to the project, and the representation of women's perceptions. This latter is not a new problem, nor one restricted to PRA research methods. PRA methods have played their part in addressing some of the gender issues in field research. In many respects, PRAs have provided good contacts in which to explore the ways in which men and women's experience, needs and perspectives differ, and innovative ways of representing these differences have been employed (Welbourn 1991, 1992; Sheelu & Devraj, 1992). For several reasons, organised group PRA exercises have not provided appropriate contexts for the articulation of women's perspectives for natural resource planning. Firstly, women faced a number of practical constraints to participation. The PRAs took place during a season when women's work does not allow participation. PRA assumed that women would be available collectively at central locations for continuous period of time. These requirements of time, locations and collective presence were incompatible with the structure of women's work roles. Women are rarely free of work responsibilities for substantial lengths of time and it is hard to find times when women would be available collectively. This imposes major constraints on women's participation.

Secondly, women faced social constraints. PRAs usually took place in public spaces and in the presence of outsiders. In a society, which ascribes to women a sphere, characterized as private domestic manual, low status informal and by implication socially less visible and valued, any event which creates processes which are perceived and understood pubic and formal tends to exclude women. Caution is needed, of course in treating 'women' as a single group. Women's access to the 'public' of the PRA would vary with age, material status, religion and class. Finally, on several occasions in early stage of PRAs when a few women were involved in PRA exercises, there were a differences in the way they responded to the tasks. Group discussions with women in one village, for example, were concerned to know about the background of the interviewer, they asked personal questions and related stories. Women felt bored by certain exercise, to tasks remained incomplete and women gave up and began communicating by singing instead. Kalpana Ram (1992) points out referring to women fish workers in South India, who are engaged in wide fish marketing networks. "The expansion of women's space which occurs in the course of practice is understood and legitimized in Mukkuvar culture only through its imperfect reference to women's cultural responsibilities as wives, mothers and daughters"

In the same way, public expressions of women's interest almost always revolve around healthcare, nutrition, domestic work and acceptable home-based income generating activities. They articulate a socially acceptable profile of women's activities. The early experience of PRA are major obstacles to women's articulation of interests in farming, natural resource management, or any other area of concern which falls beyond the publicity endorsed definition of women's roles.

A number of socio-cultural examples of 'muted ness' among women are given in the literature (Ardener, 1975, 1978; Okely 1975; Cullun, 1975). In some of these cases, women are constrained in the expression of their interests by patriarchal definition of their concerns. The influence of power on the articulation of knowledge is particularly prominent. In providing a way of thinking about the means by which these power relations influence women's communication, the theory of 'muted ness' does not, however, deny the importance of women's agency or the centrality of this in generating change. PRA will tend to emphasise formal knowledge and activities, and reinforce the invisibility of women's roles. Women do not have power necessary to represent personal concerns publicity and by default, have to conform to the categories of legitimate concern given in advance. Put another way, women have to clothe their ideas and encode their desires in particular ways to make them heard and accepted as legitimate in the public domain of the PRA. But after, their particular concerns do not find a place in the consensus, which a PRA generates, where women are concerned, much remains unsaid. This silence too may only confirm the dominant view that women have nothing to say in relation to natural resource management and thus the invisibility of their roles in this area is reinforced and communicated to outsiders. The quality of information from women is likely to increase as women become more familiar with PRA technique and more confident about articulating their perspectives (Sheelu and Deeraj, 1992). There is an important training role for PRA exercise in demonstrating the possibilities of giving formal representation—and by implication visibility and status—to women knowledge. Indeed, if the formality and public nature of PRAs initially presents obstacles to the articulation of women's perception. This problem in the methodology of PRA, once recognised, is perhaps also a key to identifying the positive role of PRA in a strategy for increasing women's profile and involvement in rural development programmes. Rural activities take place in a socially formal domain and unless women's perspectives are able to be articulated in formal terms, women will remain apart from the planning process. PRA provides one means by which women's knowledge and activities can be given formal recognition support and status, or can be transferred from the informal to the formal arena of community and project planning.

Constraints Faced by Farm Women

Rural women face different problems either on a regular basis or at different times, many of which are not easy to resolve on account of societal perceptions and other factors.

The problems can be of different kinds and they reveal them if they find opportunities for doing so. Given a chance, the rural women can describe their problems and prioritize them according to their perception.

Priortisation of Problems by Rural Women

A group of rural women in village Banstool prioritised their problems using different number of seeds. The scoring of problems brought to light different priorities of problems specified such as giving of dowry, husbands desert wives and remarry, cruelty and repression. Problem of drinking water, shortage of housing. Problem of medical treatment, wife-beating, divorce by husband, large number of children, cruelty of in-laws, shortage of land, problem of latrine, shortage of cash, harassment by fundamentalists, problem of transport etc.

Some Observations on Women's Problems

Many of the problems of rural women relate to social problems within households. These are their priority problems and most of them relate to inter-personal relationships arising from inequitable power structure within households. There are a couple of problems relating to infrastructure, some of which directly affect the workload of woman and indirectly the physical and psychological well-being of herself and her family.

Shortage of cash is a manifestation of low income and poverty and problem of land is a factor causing poverty. To top it all, the harassment by fundamentalists, which is in the nature of a religious problem is also of much consequence to the women who perceive it as a form of repression.

The social problems within households and those relating to fundamentalists arise because the women feel repressed and are not in position to assert their rights and privileges. It calls for economic and social empowerment of women whether on the basis of actions taken by state or other non-government development organizations. Formation of pressure groups of men and women in village communities or village level organizations can also play a significant role in diminishing the intensity of the stated problems. The other economic problems of finding cash and owning land are related to poverty and can be resolved through appropriate packages of poverty-reduction programmes.

Objectives
1. To study socio-economic status of farm women.
2. To study the involvement and time utilization of women in farm and home activities through PRA
3. Impact of participation of farm women in PRA technique.
4. Constraints faced by farm women in the adoption of PRA techniques during daily work.
5. To suggest suitable measures for enhancing the use of PRA techniques.

Justification of the Study

Participation is an active process in which participants can share their views and knowledge. Due to the upliftment of women in rural scenario, it is very important that they must participate in various programmes at village level.

In the case of developing countries 60 per cent people lived in villages where they are not able to find new information and techniques. And women are a main part of household activities as well as farm activities so they must be fully aware about new inventions, information or techniques.

There is a social, financial and communicational gap between men and women in village. It is believed that they are not a good planner, good organiser and good worker due to the lack of knowledge. They have less participation in decision-making due to lack of education.

So the present study "Participation of women through PRA technique" has been undertaken. As the study has been done to find out the participatory approach of women in PRA and impact on socio-economic status and living standard of women in village scenario.

The present study is also an attempt to provide new PRA techniques in farm activities and upliftment of women in rural areas through PRA among rural society.

The relevant issue in this context is first, what kind and how big are the imperfections and second, can they be overcome or minimized? Much depends on what the imperfections are and whether there are ways to bring the imperfections within reasonable limits in order to have better results from rural participation.

Each PRA exercise is unique in its own way. In each case, it starts in its own manner and proceeds in its own style based on the principles of PRA and there can be no "blue print" recommended for a PRA session. The amount of learning which takes place in a PRA exercise and the data generated vary in different situations.

Review of Literature

The review of literature is the basis of most of the research. "The literature in any field forms the foundation upon which all future work is built". Review of related literature of the study has become an established practice of all research report but this should not be taken as mere practice or traditions in writing research process. Briefly it may be pointed out that review of related literature gives an insight into the problems. The important aspect of this tradition is that the researcher comes to know about the present position of the problem and also the explored and unexplored aspect of the problem. It was in view of these considerations that the investigator shifted the pages of journals, abstracts, so the different aspect of problem may be elaborated.

Brocklesby and Holland (1998) participatory methods are flexible and diverse set of technique for visual representation and stakeholder involvement characterized by a set of underlying ethical principles.

A Time Use Study of Agricultural Farming by Women in Bangladesh (1998) represent the majority of people in the rural areas are involved in agriculture. Like men, women are also involved in agricultural farm activities in addition to household activities. Women perform different activities in and around the homestead, but usually are not involved in field operations which are usually men's work. Therefore, women's contribution to agriculture is often ignored or is not properly appreciated. But in reality they work hard to keep the farm operations running smoothly. The purpose of this study is to identify the agricultural and household activities of rural women in detail and to quantify their time allocation in a selected area of the Sherpur district of Bangladesh. The findings of the study showed that women in different farm-size groups usually took part in various agricultural and household activities. This study found that rural women keep themselves quite busy all day long. They work at least 540-660 minutes (9-11 hours) a day. Of this at least 120 minutes (2 hours) are spent for livestock and poultry rearing in homestead areas and the rest for different household activities. They do not participate directly in agricultural field activities but help in many agriculture related practices, such as post harvest operations, seed processing and kitchen gardening, which make up a significant contribution economically. The authors suggest that women's work should be properly recognized in various development activities.

L.O. Okitoi, H.O. Ondwasy and M.P. Obali (1998) Emphasis on rural poultry production has driven researchers and extensionists to develop appropriate technologies for the previously neglected area. In order for rural poultry programmes to have a positive impact on household economics and gender equity. Women's concerns have to be integrated in the programmes as a gender variable. This requires a more explicit understanding of gender issues in rural poultry production system. Gender specific roles and responsibilities are often conditioned by a household structure and success to resources.

Praxis (1999) PRAs having been made it clear that the realities and priorities of poor people are often different from those supposed for them by the professionals and policy makers. One of the major challenges in PRA has been to enable the realities and priorities of the poor and marginalized people to be expressed and communicated to policy makers.

Kunwar Neelma (2000) PRA is a rapidly evolving branch of knowledge and has the potential to make people active participants in development initiative. Robert Chambers has defined PRA as a family of approaches and methods of enable rural people to present share and analyse their knowledge of life and conditions to plan and act. It can be viewed as a shift from closed to open, verbal to visual, individual to group, measuring to comparing. In simple terms it makes the local community the central actors in a development initiative. It is a tool used by the community chiefly for the following purpose.

Kunwar Neelma (2000) PRA is seen as most appropriate in terms of collective thinking and action which is geared towards sustainable development and taking new information collectively. Development from 'within' requires the rural community to develop a new literacy. This kind of literacy would enable local people to analyze their own socio-economic problems and resources to combat poverty.

Kunwar Neelma (2000) participatory research has comes distinguishing characteristics, which focus process, collaboration, and problem solving and knowledge generation. All these characteristics help mobilize community to be active partners in shaping their own destiny. The philosophical rooting of PR are embedded in empowering the community by making them central to any knowledge generation process which would eventually feed into an action programme meant for betterment of the community involved in the research process.

Pratt Garett (2001) PRA can generate space and time for communication in the community. It allows for the construction of bridges between those subjects involved who participate in project, between communities and state institutions.

Kimanzi (2001) explains the changes that have happened as the NGO World Neighbours has applied PRA in a Kenyan community. The story illustrates the way that PRA is practiced in particular circumstances and is entangled in complex process of social change. PRA is only a small part of world neighbours' on going interactions with the communities where they work, alongside extension activities, organization building, and liaison with government officials.

Jone and Speech (2001) document how participating in PRA can change the way people behave in other situations. When Speech practices PRA, they create a temporary social space with its own norms or rules for proper behaviour that are different from those governing everyday social spaces. These rules include for example, that women should speak as equals to men in these spaces and that any views expressed should be considered on their own merit.

Holmes (2001) have studied that field workers in Action Aid. The Gambia (AATG) understand and use PRA. They receive the same guidance and policy message. They are under the same organizational preservers facing similar workloads, deadlines, and budgetary cycle. They also face similar social pressures as they negotiate relationship with people in the different ways. Some think it should be done every six months, others say every five years. Some think communities should be divided into subgroups for PRA, while others think the whole community should meet together. Few uses PRA tools for subsequent updates to community actions plans. As Holmes argues, individual field agents take the initiative to do PRA and their other duties in ways that make sense to them, given their background, personal objectives and understanding of their role. As much as managers try to impart one idea of how to do PRA. Correctly each field worker will interpret and practice it in their own way.

Singh (2001) conducted studies which reflects on the global spread of PRA and on factors that enabled it to spread so rapidly. One was the personal excitement and learning generated by the use of PRA methods. Another was the important role played by a first generation of 'Champions' and trainers and their contribution to supporting a second generation. He also argues that the space made for continuing innovation made it possible for many people to be pioneering in their own right as they picked up PRA and made it their own. National and international networking and flows of information about PRA worked together and practices and with each other, open ended support from powerful global actors allowed decentralized. Loose global networking. He ends on a cautionary note. The financial rewards and 'culture of consultancy' that have come with PRA's popularity may underline continued sharing and learning. As PRA is used more widely, there is a risk that the underlying values will erode, he suggests that continued critical reflection may be one way forward.

Muthengi (2001) explains the changes that have happened as NGO world neighbours have applied PRA in a Kenyon community. The story illustrates the way that PRA is practiced in particular circumstances and is entangled in complex processes of social change, PRA is only a small part of world neighbours on going interactions with the communities here they work, alongside extension activities, organization building and liaison with government officials.

John R. Campbell (2001) Anthropologists and many others are making increasing use of participatory research methods in a variety of applied contexts. While aware of the potential advantages of such methods, this paper outlines a number of methodological issues that need to be carefully considered. Such issues, when taken together with the problem of combining participatory with qualitative and quantitative research, argue strongly not only for caution in using the methods but also for the need to undertake basic research on participatory methods themselves. This paper looks at the development of participatory rural appraisal (PRA) in development research, and critically examines three methods—interviewing, visualization and ranking/scoring—in terms of their relation to established qualitative research. It then turns to the problems that arise from using PRA techniques. Finally, the validity and reliability of PRA are discussed in relation to arguments about sequencing/

triangulating research techniques, an argument which is shown to be as problematic as the unexamined use of PRA.

Mukherjee (2002) represented that PRA/PLA type activities involves teamwork and analysis by both insiders and outsiders. For PRA/PLA type activities some spade work is essential so as to enable adequate background preparation and follow up exercises. There are tools and methods fostering better understanding of the topics to be probed better preparation and analyse, garnering team sprit and team work so as to improve the quality of PRA/PLA.

Kunwar Neelma and Vashishtha Priya (2003) said that represented that Participatory Rural Appraisal (PRA) is a methodology for interacting with villagers, understanding them and learning from them. It involves a set of principles, a process of communication and a menu of method for seeking villager's participation in putting forward their points of view about any issue and enabling them do their own analysis with a view to make use of such learning. It initiates a participatory process and sustains it. Its principles and the menu of methods help in organizing participation.

Lauren Starr (2003) women have never enjoyed equal representation in Canadian politics. Since their federal enfranchisement in 1921, women have rarely become actively involved in politics. Not only were female candidates unsuccessful, there were many elections that did not include a single female candidate. Until the 1980s, political representation of women was below twelve per cent all across Canada. Presently, there are 63 women in the House of Commons out of a possible three hundred and one seats. While the gap between men and women MPs is much smaller than it ever was, 21 per cent is not equality. To understand why women continue to make up less than 50 per cent of the federal or provincial legislatures, it is helpful to explore the uniqueness of the women who overcame political exclusion in Canada in the twentieth century.

Jamal and Arya (2004) represented that participatory Rural Appraisal method has been considered the most appropriate to understand and analyse the local situations. Proper understanding of the farmers and livestock owners, their situations, problems and solutions from their point of view has always been the challenge before the scientists, and extension workers development workers, especially in democratic countries like ours.

West Bank/Gaza Sep. 2004 – Oct. 2004 TANGO worked with CARE and partner organizations to undertake an assessment of the conditions systems, risks and opportunities related to the livelihood security and rights realization of the poorest and most vulnerable households and groups in the Occupied Palestinian Territories. As part of this assignment, TANGO provided training to CARE and partner agency staff in the understanding and application of Household Livelihood Security and rights-based concepts, as well as participatory assessment methodologies.

A.K. Mishra, K.V. Subrahmanyam (2004) represented that small ruminants are essential component of rainfed farming systems in semi-arid India. Two models of sheep rearing, lamb fattening and breed multiplication were promoted as a source of income generation and self-employment for the poor and landless households in clusters of two/three selected villages in Mahabubnagar and Anantapur district of Andhra Pradesh and Tumkur district of Karnataka, India. *Salaha Samithi* (farmers advisory committee) facilitated implementation and monitoring of intervention. The core principle of the process was active, decision-making involvement of people at all stages of technology development with technical input and facilitation by project staff. Exposure visits and dialogue are used as a guiding principle, involving open discussion among farmers, NGO workers and research.

Jerome Destombes (2004) In tropical and labour-intensive pleasant economies, agriculture and livelihoods follow sharp seasonal patterns whereby food supplies are at a through when labour demand peaks in order to meet heavy farming schedules as the rainy season starts. This paper takes experiences of, and vulnerabilities to, seasonal hunger as vantage point to investigate the rationale and if so the scope, for customizing poverty alleviation to the distinctive sets of constraints faced by different socio-economic groups in rural sub-Saharan Africa.

Thelma Paris (2004) The results of the PRA showed that the proportion of households with migrants is higher in Thailand than in the Philippines and Vietnam. A higher proportion of males than females migrate in Thailand and Vietnam and vice versa in the Philippines. The incidence of out-migration is generally higher in rainfed ecosystems than in irrigated ecosystems. Rural to urban migration is prevalent in Thailand and Vietnam because of more employment opportunities in nearby districts and provinces brought about by rapid industrialization and better communication and transportation facilities. In the Philippines, although rural to urban migration occurs, domestic to international migration is more prevalent. In Vietnam, men work as construction workers and masons in the cities and as hired fishermen, in sea fishing and with shrimp or squid catching in other provinces. Women work in waste trading and small trading, as hired labourers in rice farming, sand beating workers, domestic helpers, and factory workers, or in other industrial areas near rural areas. In Thailand, male and female migrants work as construction workers, factory workers and in the trading/business and service sector.

Thelma Paris (2004) Women cooperators were trained in the use of these technologies. In Vietnam, before the training, women were given tests on their existing knowledge on pest identification, weed management, cultural practices to maintain healthy plants, reduce inputs and high yield as well as the methods of pest control. Leaflets (about 1000) which include the important roles of women in rice farming were also distributed in the communes and villages.

Hindu Kush-Himalaya (2004) represented the promotion of rural enterprises is crucial for the achievement of broader development objectives, including poverty alleviation, economic development and the promotion of more democratic and pluralist societies in mountain regions. Transformation of mountain economies from subsistence to market orientation and diversification into activities based on the special advantages offered by mountain regions for producing high value and value added commodities is essential for improving the livelihoods of the rural poor in the mountain regions. The International Centre for Integrated Mountian Development (ICIMOD) studies have shown that niche-based mountain products and services, including horticultural products, medicinal herbs, non-timber forest products (NTFP's), livestock products, silk fibres, crafts, beekeeping products and mountain tourism, can serve as a basis for diversifying the incomes of rural mountain communities in the Hindu Kush Himalayas.

FAO Corporate Document Repository (2004) In the region, diverse technical line ministries serve as agencies of change to address the concerns of rural women as actors in agriculture and the rural economy and as stakeholders in rural communities. Ministries of agriculture, livestock, fisheries, environment and irrigation and rural development are examples of technical line ministries. The trend has been to create focal units or focal persons for gender or women within these technical line ministries, though with limited interaction among the various focal persons in the discrete line ministries. Consequently, the institutional situation remains with parallel structures to achieve objectives associated with the advancement of women and development in rural areas. Agencies focussed on gender equality and women follow the agenda for gender equality, women's empowerment and advancement of women.

Adewumi, Olaniyi Matthew A fundamental challenge the world faces today is ensuring that millions of households living in poverty have access to enough food to maintain a healthy life. Africa over the years has been looking for ways to solving the problem of food security and it is an important topic in discussions of Africa leaders. While there are national data on food security and poverty, information on rural food security and poverty are not readily available especially in Nigeria. This study, therefore, employed discriminant analysis to examine the levels and the major determinants of food security and poverty among the rural households who are the major producers of food in Nigeria.

Door E. Revath (2004) The social consequence of suicides is immense on the deceased household. The pressure of unpaid debts remained on the women persistently. Delayed payment of relief from government though was useful in settlement of debts but in most cases it also witnessed sale of assets unable to bear the pressure of debts. Kinship, community, local governance, political parties intervened to some extent in settlement of debts and in reducing the pressure of repayment, phasing it and also waiving or standardizing the interest rate. In the pre suicide situation most women used to work in the farm as wage labour or in their own farm. But in the post suicide situation as cultivator they had to own up the entire responsibility of running it or as agriculture labour had to diversify to casual wage work to support the family. Women belonging to the middle and lower social groups wound up most of the debts with help of government relief package, leased out land and took to wage labour thereby slipping into unstable occupations and incomes. Where they took up cultivation it was a difficult task in terms of lack of extension, information of markets, interface with markets etc. Besides, the insufficient infrastructure in terms of power, irrigation also puts them to innumerable difficulties.

Report Livelihood Assessment and Microfinance Programme (2004-05) presented poverty is a complex concept and process characterized by low income, poor health, low literacy level, under nutrition and inadequate housing and living condition, lack of access to credit. It is also widely accepted fact that poverty has a gender bias as 70 per cent of the people living in abject poverty are women. A high proportion of coastal fishing community is poor. The approach and mission of micro-finance is helping poor to move out of poverty.

Arjun, K. Sengupta (2005) In the report, the commission notes that the situation calls for immediate steps to ensure minimum conditions of work for the unorganized workers as well as measures for their livelihood promotion. The commission has, therefore, proposed two comprehensive bills for unorganized agricultural and non-agricultural workers. It has, further, proposed a number of measures to improve the livelihood of unorganized sector workers.

Canegrowers' Strategy for Women and Teams (15 Sept. 2006) Women are a critical part of the farm management team in Australian agriculture. With 98 per cent of Australia's farm businesses run by farm families (Gaurnaut and Lim-Applegate 1998), women are a significant part of the agricultural workforce. Often, however, the contribution of women is invisible. As illustrated by Pini, while this is the case in the sugar industry, it is also across most agricultural industries.

National Women's Council of Ireland, National Strategy Plan (NSP) 2007-2013. (January 2006) It is imperative that in forthcoming rural development strategy these women are counted as being part of rural Ireland and specifically that women who experience poverty and social exclusion are specifically named and targeted to benefit from the development that will result from the strategy's implementation.

Azad India Foundation (2006) Different sectors of economy have different experiences about the impact of the reforms. In a country like India, productive employment is central to poverty reduction strategy and to bring about economic equality in the society. But the results of unfettered operation of market forces are not always equitable, especially in India, where some groups are likely to be subjected to disadvantage as a result of globalization. Women constitute one such vulnerable group.

Rabert Chambers (2006) PRA originally stood for participatory Rural Appraisal, but its applications are in many, many contexts besides rural, and good practice is empowering and for more than just appraisal. PLA stands for participatory learning and action. As a term it is often used interchangeably with PRA.

Raphael Abiodun Olawepo (2007) reported fish production and marketing are as old as the rural communities involved in the lucrative occupation in Badagry area of Lagos State, Nigeria. A random sampling of 200 fishermen using Participatory Rural Appraisal techniques (PRA) in five Badagry villages was used to explore coastal fishing and socio-economic development in the study area with a view to enhancing local productivity and sustainability. The findings show that an average fisherman in Badagry is aware of the resources available in his environment, and can affect productivity levels positively if given adequate incentives. There are two lessons from this study; one has to do with what PRA tells us about the fishing community, the other is the importance of facilitators that have, amongst other things, good listening skills. The experience also revealed that field workers' ability to listen and learn from local fishermen was a critical factor in collecting in-depth information that could be used for rural community planning.

Participatory Rural Appraisal (PRA) techniques participatory mapping (2007). Mapping exercise as used in a PRA activity not only provide the evaluator with information about the physical characteristics of the community, but can also reveal much about the socio-economic conditions and how the participants perceive their community. The maps are usually drawn by a group of villagers either on the ground using chalk or on a large sheet of paper. The exercise often attracts much attention and generates useful debate among the mapmakers and the onlookers. The final map is then recorded by the PRA team to use in subsequent discussions.

Kiranjot Sidhu (2007) represented post harvesting is an important component of farm activities and is mostly performed by women. They play a vital role in subsequent processing and storage of the produce. In order to understand the present participation pattern of farm women in post harvest activities an attempt was made under the Extension component of All India Coordinated Research Project on Home Science. The study conducted on 2999 farm families in rural Punjab represented by five agro-climatic zones and five distinct landholding categories clearly indicate an active participation of women in most of the selected activities in the area of post harvesting. The results varied between zones but the women were found to contribute substantially in drying, storage and cleaning. In other activities majority of the women were working with male members. However, least participation was reported in processing and marketing. Study points towards a need to technically arm women in post harvest know-how so as to help in reducing losses during storage. This shall not only reduce economic losses but help in maintaining family food security.

Interactive Multimedia Compact Disc (IMCD) (2007) Women are now playing a pivotal role in all fields, including agriculture, as managers, decision makers and skilled farm workers. It is estimated that women are responsible for 70 per cent of actual farm work and constitute up to 60 per cent of the farming population. They are considered to be 'agripreneurs' as they supervise, organize and assure responsibilities for running both their farm and households. In spite of all these efforts, it is most unfortunate to note that involvement and participation of farm women in Transfer of Technology (ToT) has been neglected so far. Hence, it is the need of the hour to empower farm women in technology dissemination programmes to achieve a holistic empowerment of society.

International Development Research Centre (2007) The researchers compared the village farm management techniques with the principles of sustainable agriculture and found the village techniques to be characteristic of low-external-input and sustainable agriculture. Villagers managed the soil and maintained crop health by imitating local ecological processes. The indigenous beliefs and practices were examined in relation to people's resource use and conservation. The beliefs associated with the use of trees and animals placed temporary or permanent restrictions on their use. An informal system of religious and spiritual taboos, the local customs and the fear of community sanctions.

Hillsborough County Farm Bureau (Sep. 8, 2007) The Hillsborough County Farm Bureau Women's Committee is involved in many different projects with a focus on agriculture education and promotion. Some of the Women's Committee projects are, the youth speech contest, where our country winner will go on to represent us at the district level and then hopefully at the state contest. Ag-Venture is another project that our women's committee works with it is an opportunity for us to tell the story of our farming operations to third graders in Hillsborough County. The Hillsborough County Women's Committee is also very proud to sponsor and judge the youth open baking and craft show at the Florida Strawberry Festival each year. These are just a few of our projects. We invite you to come and join us.

Improve Integrated Dairy Production (21 Sep., 2007) describes the rationale and importance of the approaches and methodologies of Participatory Rural Appraisal (PRA) to enable constraint analysis, to understand the complexities of farming systems and to improve integrated dairy productivity. Implicit in this objective is Farming System Research (RSR), which focussed on cropping systems in the 1970's, with the subsequent addition of animal components. The methodology for FSR involves the following sequential components; site selection, site description and characterization (diagnosis), planning of on-farm research, on-farm testing and validation of alternatives, diffusion of results, and impact assessment. PRA is the development of FSR, which involves the active participation of farmers to identify constraints and plan appropriate solutions. In the Coordinated Research Project (CRP), the approach was adapted to 10 different country situations and led to Economic Opportunity Surveys (EOS) and Diagnostic Surveillance Studies (DSS), allowing the planning and implantation of integrated interventions of improve dairy productivity.

Rural Cooperatives (Nov-Dec. 2007) represented if any of the rural women felt remotely unnecessary to cooperatives, the thought was quickly dispelled at the various sessions on women's involvement. Women have the opportunity to be an influential force in cooperatives, particularly those 60,000 to 75,000 who are wives of managers and directors said women Halberg. AIC President, Keynoter of the women's workshop.

Jadabaranda Panda (2007) Senior Faculty It is a general belief in many cultures that the role of women is to build and maintain the homely affairs like task of fetching water, cooking and rearing children. Since the turn of the century, the status of women in India has been changing due to growing industrialization, urbanization, spatial mobility and social legislation. With the spread of education awareness, women have shifted from kitchen to higher level of professional activities.

IAAS World Congress in Belarus (2008) The concept village programme managed by IAAS is known as Village Concept Project. Kondangmerak Village (Malang Regency) was selected as the most potential village, compared to the two other candidate villages, that is, Ranupane and Banurejo, considering that the village is quite near and it has limited human resources and infrastructures. Some of its potencies to be explored optimally, according to Dwi, are its being a natural tourist beach, it's a lot of reef, the fact that it has not enjoyed electricity, and its various potencies to be developed.

Workshop ISTECS : Towards the Sustainable Agricultural Development (2008), The workshop was accompanied by Focus Group Discussion (FGD) that aimed at analyzing various latest agricultural problems in Indonesia, and to help Indonesian government formulate the solution to those problems. The participants of this event were Indonesian students who are now studying in various universities in Germany, such as, Goettingen, Kassel and Stuttgart.

Eka Nugraha, S.Pt. (2008) describes related to food and agricultural problems, he suggested finding a solution, figuring out ways to make farmers get advantages by empowering farmers and promoting agriculture. In particular, he exemplified the Japanese mode of agriculture that was enormous support from the government through price protection, irrigation projects and high yielding seed provision.

CIDA China Programme (2008) it is a process through which the women and men most effected by CIDA's development programming participate in determining both the means and the results of the programming. Participatory development is not necessary achieved only by having large numbers of people attend meetings and trainings; rather, opportunities in which women and men can themselves act as agents of change need to be facilitated.

Gender and Development Plan of Action (2008-2013) represented that gender equality gains are essential to fulfill FAO's mandate of raising levels of nutrition and standards of living and improve agricultural productivity and livelihoods of rural populations. Gender roles and relations are of key importance to understanding and overcoming challenges to improving livelihoods in development and emergency contexts. Nevertheless, women and girls continue to face limited access to and control over, productive resources, and agricultural responses have traditionally been neither sufficiently aware of, more responsive to the distinct roles, priorities, knowledge, constraints and opportunities of women as compared to men. Thus, there is a continued need to mainstream gender concerns into FAO projects, programmes and policies, as well as to assist member countries of mainstream gender equality and enhance their capacity to analyse and address gender-related development challenges.

CHAPTER 3

Profile of the Study Area

Prior to discuss the findings of the study on "Participation of farmwomen through PRA technique", it is essential to sketch briefly the salient features of the study area. The following are the brief features of district Kanpur.

District Kanpur

Kanpur is said to be the corruption of Kanhaiyapur or Kanhpur, which was an unimportant village till its first contact with the British. According to a local tradition, the name of Kanhpur Kohna owes its origin to Hindu Singh, Raja of Sachendi, who came here about 1750, to bathe in the holy river, the Ganga and established a village, which he (possibly) named Kanhpur, the name becoming changed to Kanpur in the course of time.

Location

The district of Kanpur occupies the north-western part of the Allahabad division and belongs to the tract known as the lower doab (which comprises the eastern extremity of the strip of country lying between the Ganga and the Yamuna rivers). In shape, it is an irregular quadrilateral and lies between the parallel of $25^0 26'$ and $26^0 58'$ north latitude and $70^0 31'$ and $80^0 34'$ east longitude. To the north-east, beyond the Ganga, the deep stream of which forms the boundary of the district, lie the districts of Hardoi and Unnao, while to the south, across the Yamuna, are the districts of Hamirpur and Jalaun. On the south-east , the boundary marches with that of Bindki (a tahsil of Fatehpur) and to the west and north-west are the Auraiya and Bidhuna tahsils of district Auraiya and that of Kannauj district.

Area

According to the Central Statistical Organization, the district had an area of 3015 Sq.km. (Census, 2001) with 1040 Sq.km. area covered under Kanpur district, from which four zones were selected for the present study.

Population

According to the census of 2001, the district had a population of 25,51,337 in which 13,74,121 are males and 11,77,216 are females and occupied the 2nd position in the state in respect of population.

Sub-divisions Tahsils

The district has six sub-divisions – Bilhaur, Derapur, Bhognipur, Akbarpur, Kanpur and Ghatampur, each having a tahsil of the same name.

The Kanpur tahsil lies in the east of the district. It is bounded on the east and north-east by district Unnao, the Ganga demarcating the boundary between the two districts. On its north-west is tahsil Bilhaur, on the west is tahsil Akbarpur and on the south is tahsil Ghatampur and district Fatehpur. According to the census of 1991, it had 279 villages and 2 towns covering an area of 1040 sq.km. with a population of 24,18,487 persons (females 10,92,759). There are total 10 blocks in Kanpur tahsil.

Topography

Like the rest of the doab, the district generally constitutes an alluvial plain, which slopes gradually from north-west to south-east, the slope following the line of the main rivers.

This plain is somewhat undulating because of the many subsidiary watersheds that intersperse the minor drainage lines. The sectional contour is almost the same, the level rising sharply from the bed of the Ganga to the crest of the high cliff and then sloping gently towards the centre, beyond which it once again ascends to the ridge, which overlooks the valley of the Yamuna. The same phenomenon occurs on a smaller scale in the case of the minor rivers in the district but where the watercourse has a small volume and little velocity, the change in the level is hardly perceptible.

RIVER SYSTEM AND WATER RESOURCES

Rivers

The two chief rivers of the district are the Ganga and the Yamuna. The Isan and the Non are the tributaries of the Ganga and the Rind and Sengar are the chief tributaries of the Yamuna. The river next in importance is the Pandu.

Ganga

The Ganga enters the village of Chita-Mau and flows along the north-eastern and eastern boundaries of the district for its entire length and also skirts the Bilhaur and Kanpur tahsil. It has a wide and sandy bed, changing its channel almost every year, as its sand-banks are formed and washed away. In the rains, the Ganga is of immense breadth, but during the cold weather it shrinks to much smaller dimensions. Along its banks there is generally a narrow strip of recent alluvium, but in most cases, the soil is almost pure sand. Above the sandy foreshore rises the Ganga cliff, which consists of a high ridge running in an almost continuous line throughout the district. The river leaves the district at village Purwa Mir in the Kanpur tahsil.

Yamuna

The Yamuna first touches this district in the extreme west of Bhognipur and maintains a south-easterly course. It makes many loops and bends and leaves the district in the extreme south-west of the Ghatampur tahsil. It separates this district from the Jalaun and Hamirpur districts in the south. The bed of the river is at a considerable depth below the level of the land to the north and in places there are many fertile stretches between the river and its high bank.

Lakes

The district has a large number of small depressions in which surface water collects to form shallow jhils. The important ones being found in the south of Bilhaur in Akbarpur, in northern Ghatampur and in parts of the Kanpur tahsil.

Climate

The climate of the district is characterized by a hot summer and general dryness except in the south-west monsoon season. The year may be divided into four seasons. The period from March to about the middle of June is the summer season, which is followed by the south-west monsoon season which lasts till about the end of September, October and the first half of November forms the post-monsoon or transition period. The cold season spreads from about the middle of November to February.

Rainfall

Records of rainfall in the district are available for 8 stations for periods ranging from 51 to 97 years. The average annual rainfall in the district is 778.9 mm (30.67") The rainfall in the district varies from 642.3 mm (25.29") at Narwal to 884.8 mm (34.83") at Kanpur. About 89 per cent of the annual rainfall is received during the monsoon months (June to September) August being the rainiest month. The variation in the annual rainfall from year to year is appreciable. In the fifty-year period, 1901 to 1950, the highest annual rainfall, which was 155 per cent of the normal, occurred in 1904. The lowest annual rainfall, 43 per cent of the normal, occurred in 1918. In this fifty-year period, the annual rainfall in the district was less than 80 per cent of the normal in 12 years, none of which were consecutive. Considering the rainfall at individual stations, two consecutive years of such low rainfall occurred three times at Bilhaur, Akbarpur and Ghatampur and twice at Kanpur and Bhognipur and 3 consecutive years of such low rainfall occurred once at Bilhaur.

Temperature

There is a meteorological observatory at Kanpur and the records of this observatory may be taken as representative of the climatic conditions prevailing in the district in general. About the beginning of March there is a rapid rise in temperature. May and the early part of June constitute the hottest part of the year. The mean daily maximum temperature in May is 41.3^0C (106.3^0F) or above. Hot, dry and dust laden westerly winds are common in the hot season. Afternoon thundershowers, which occur a few times during the summer, bring temporary relief. With the onset of monsoon after the middle of June, the day temperature drops appreciably. Nights continue to be as warm as those during the latter part of the summer. Towards the end of the monsoon (in September and in October) there is a slight increase in the day temperature but the nights temperatures decrease rapidly. January is generally the coldest month with the mean daily maximum temperature at 22.3°C (72.1°F) and the mean daily minimum at 7.8°C (16.0°F). During the cold season, in association with passing western disturbances, cold waves affect the district and the minimum temperature drops down to about the freezing point of water and frost occurs.

The highest maximum and the lowest maximum temperature recorded in the years 1996-97 and 1997-98 were 44.2°C and 0.7°C, respectively.

Humidity

During the monsoon season, the humidity generally exceeds 70 per cent but after that is decreases. The driest part of the year is the summer season when in the afternoon the humidity is less than 30 per cent.

DISTRIBUTION BETWEEN URBAN AND RURAL AREA

(*a*) **Kanpur Tahsil :** There are total 10 blocks in Kanpur tahsil namely – Kalyanpur, Vidhunu, Sarsaul, Chaubepur, Shivrajpur, Bilhaur, Kakvan, Patara, Bheetargaon and Ghatampur. Out of these 10 blocks, the two blocks Kalyanpur and Sarsaul were chosen for the study.

(*b*) **Villages selected :** From two blocks Kalyanpur 5 villages Singhpur, Prempur, Ishwariganj, Gangapur and Gambhirpur and 5 villages Tilsehri, Pali, Phuphuwar, Tajpur and Bausar were selected from Sarsaul block.

Research Methodology

This chapter deals with the research procedures applied in conducting the present study. For convenience, the research methodology has been discussed under the following three sub-heads.

(*i*) Locale of the study

(*ii*) Sampling procedure

(*iii*) Selection of variables

(*iv*) Operationalisation of variables and their empirical measurement

(*v*) Construction of interview schedule

(*vi*) Data collection

(*vii*) Statistical analysis

(*i*) Locale of the Study

Uttar Pradesh was chosen as locale of the study. This was done with the intension that U.P. is a major state of the country and men and women have an important role to play in the development of the state as well as the country. Besides, number of schemes being implemented in the state was another reason to carryout this study in Uttar Pradesh.

(*ii*) District under Study

District Kanpur was deliberately selected for this study as the researcher hailed from this place. This helped the

DISTRICT- KANPUR

Map 4.1

investigator to collect the necessary information accurately and timely. The researcher, being from the same place could easily have dialogues and discussion with the respondents both during pilot study and final data collection.

(iii) Selection of Blocks

District Kanpur comprises of ten blocks, out of which two blocks namely, Kalyanpur and Sarsaul were randomly selected for the purpose of drawing sample. Two blocks were sufficient number of villages for indicated size of sample could be drawn.

(iv) Villages Identified for the Study

In order to identify sufficient number of villages for drawing an appropriate size of samples, a list of total villages falling in the block was prepared separately. From the block ten villages situated at a distance were selected with the help of systematic random sampling method. Thus, a total of ten villages were selected for the purpose of drawing the sample of respondents.

(v) Selection of Respondents

After having prepared a list of respondent's family separately for all the ten villages, 24 women were identified from each of the one village making a total sample of 240 respondents for the present study.

B. VARIABLES AND THEIR OPERATIONALIZATION

1. Independent Variables

(i) **Socio-economic features :** The socio-economic features of the farm women in the present study was operationalized in terms of the independent variables like age, family type, caste, type of farm women, education, economic status, occupation, income, type of house, material possession. A schedule was developed to measure these sub-concepts in order to arrive at the actual social and economic status of the farm women.

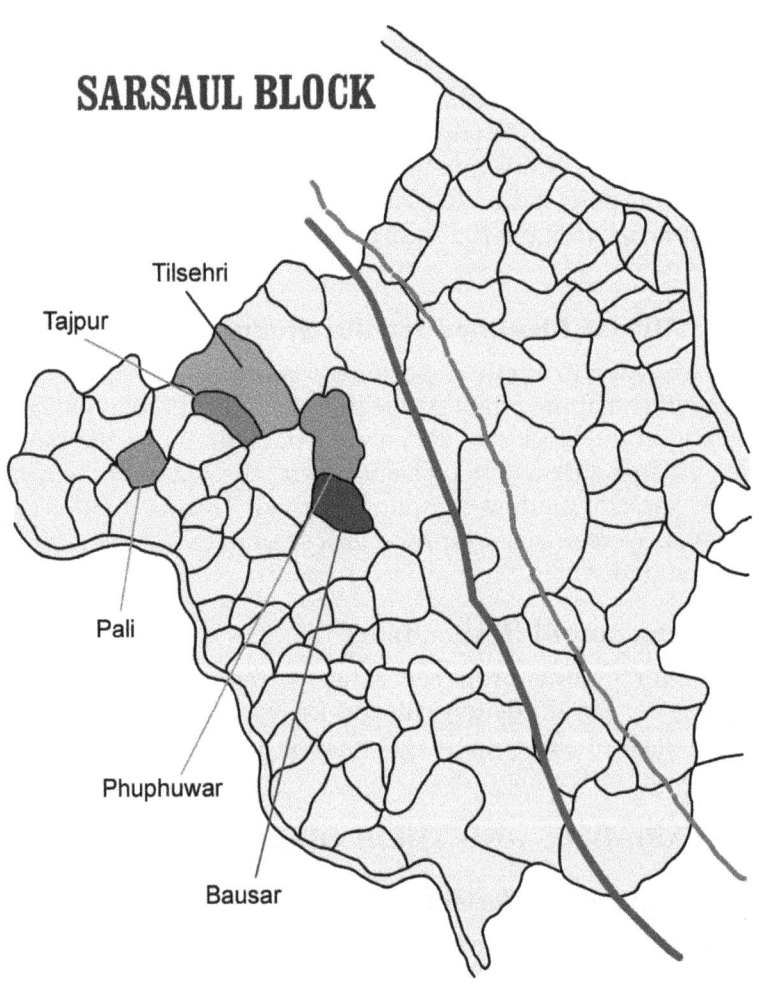

Map 4.2

(*a*) **Age** : Age is defined as the chronological age of respondents in form of number of completed years.

Age-group	Score assigned
25 to 30 years	1
30 to 40 years	2
40 to 50 years	3
50 and above	4

(*b*) **Family structure** : Family composition was scored on the basis of

(*a*) According to family type	Score assigned
Nuclear	1
Joint	2
(*b*) According to family members	Score assigned
Upto 5 members	1
Above 5 members	2

(*c*) **Caste** : Caste of the respondents in the study was measrued on the basis of response of individual women to which they belong i.e. in terms of upper caste, middle caste and lower caste.

Caste	Score assigned
Upper	1
O.B.C.	2
S.C.	3

(*d*) **Type of farm women** : The following scoring pattern was adopted for type of farmwomen.

Women	Score assigned
Landless	1
Marginal	2
Small	3
Large	4

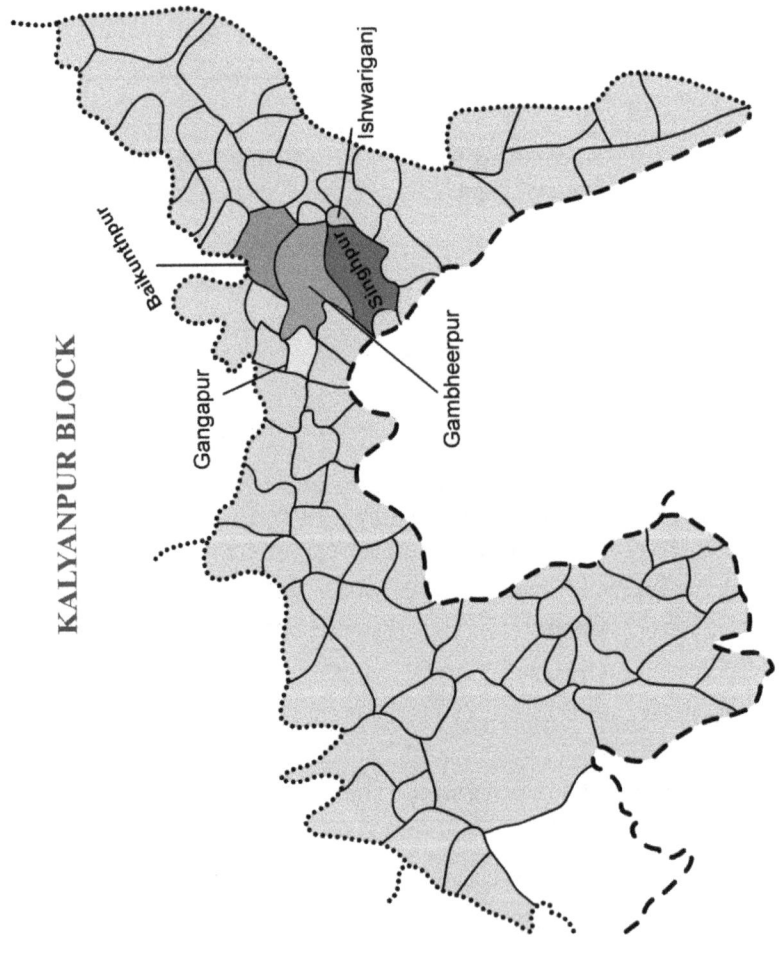

(e) **Education** : Education refers to the schooling education one has achieved. Educational satus of the respondents was measured as per scoring system followed in socio-economic status scale of Trivedi (1963) with certain modifications.

Level of education	Score assigned
Illiterate	1
Up to Primary	2
Up to Secondary	3
High School	4
Intermediate and above	5

(f) **Economic status** : The following scoring pattern was adopted for type of economic status.

Economic status	Score assigned
Earner	1
Helper	2
Dependent	3

(g) **Occupation** : This was measured on the basis of the scores allotted to different family occupation.

Occuption	Score assigned
Landless	1
Caste occupation	2
Farming	3
Business	4
Service	5

(h) **Income** : This was earned by the respondent. The score was assigned as :

Monthly income	Score assigned
Up to Rs. 1500	1
Rs. 1501 – 3000	2
Rs. 3001 – 4500	3
Rs. 4501 – 6000	4
Rs. 6001 and above	5

(*i*) **Family income :** It is the sum of income earned by all the members of the family. The score on income assigned in the following way :

Income category	Score assigned
Up to Rs. 50,000	1
Rs. 50001 and above	2

(*j*) **House type :** The house of respondents were categorized and score were assigned as :

Type of house	Score assigned
Kaccha	1
Pacca	2
Mixed	3

(*k*) **Material possession :** This was measured on the basis of the scroes allotted to different material possession :

Material possession	Score assigned
Up to 5 items	1
6 to 10 items	2
11 items and above	3

II. Dependent Variables

(*a*) **PRA :** Participatory Rural Appraisal (PRA) is a methodology for interacting with villagers, understanding them and learning from them. It involves a set of principles a process of communication and a menu of method for seeking villagers participation in putting forward their points of view about any issue and enabling them do their own analysis with a view to make use of such learning. It initiates a participatory process and sustain it. Its principle and menu of method help in organizing participation.

(*b*) **Role of women :** Role of women in farm operations, animal husbandry operation and household activities was calculated as

Dominating role	-	More than 66 per cent of total work performed

Supporting role   -   33 – 65 per cent of total work performed

No role   -   No work is performed

The involvement and time spent by women in farm, animal husbandry and domestic operations have also been assessed.

(c) **Participation** : The people define participation as a voluntary contribution in one or another of the public programmes supposed to contribute to national development, but the people are not expected to take part in shaping the programme or in criticizing its contents.

(d) **Utilization** : It refers to the full use of an available resource at the part of the client called utilization.

(e) **Technology** : The term technology is derived from Greek word 'Techneos'. Technology is the application of scientific principles and theories in behavioural term for human welfare.

(f) **Involvement** : It refers to include in any activity or person participate in any activity by own interests.

(g) **Constraints** : It refers to something which limits the achievements of an objective. It may be of a biological, economic, social, cultural, personal, resource or other nature.

Time of Investigation

The data collection was initiated from 9 October 2007 to 9 July, 2008.

Hypotheses

Ho : There is no relationship between time utilization and involvement of farm women through PRA technique.

Ho : There is no relationship between independent variables and impact of participation in various activities of farm women.

Statistical Measurement

The following statistical methods were used in the study based on the nature of data and relevant information.

(*a*) **Percentage :** Simple comparisons were made on the basis of percentage. For drawing the frequency of a particular cell is multiplied by 100 and divided by total number of observations in that particular category to which they belonged.

Symbolically percentage of the cell

$$= \frac{K}{T} \times 100$$

Where,

K is the frequency of the cell

T is the number of total observation

(*b*) **Weighted mean :** It is average which is calculated on the basis of weights and coding. If $X_1, X_2, X_3, \ldots\ldots X_n$, are the codes and $W_1 + W_2 + W_3 \ldots\ldots W_n$ are their respective weights, then :

$$\text{Weighted mean} = \frac{W_1 X_1 + W_2 X_2 + W_3 X_3 + \ldots W_n X_n}{W_1 + W_2 + W_3 \ldots W_n}$$

$$= \sum_{i=1}^{n} \frac{W_i X_i}{W_i}$$

(*c*) **'t' test :** The significant difference between two sample mean :

$$t = \frac{[\bar{X}_1 - \bar{X}_2]}{\sqrt{\sigma_c^2 [1/n_1 + 1/n_2]}}$$

$$\sigma_c^2 = \frac{\Sigma (X_1 - \bar{X}_2)^2 + \Sigma (X_2 - \bar{X}_2)^2}{(n_1 - 1) + (n_2 - 1)}$$

σ_c^2 = pooled estimate variance

$\bar{X}_1$ = mean of the first sample

$\bar{X}_2$ = mean of the second sample

(*d*) **Correlation coefficient (*r*) :** The correlation between two variables, in which one is dependent on other, was calculated by product moment method, which is as—

$$r = \frac{\text{Cov.}(X.Y)}{\sqrt{\text{Var.}(X).\text{Var.}(Y)}}$$

or

$$r = \frac{n\Sigma xx_i y_i - (\Sigma x_i)(\Sigma y_i)}{\sqrt{[n\Sigma x_i^2 - (\Sigma x_i)^2]^{1/2}[n\Sigma y_i^2 - (\Sigma y_i)^2]^{1/2}}}$$

The correlation coefficient was tested with t-test for its significance as

$$t = \frac{r\sqrt{n-2}}{\sqrt{1-r^2}}$$

The calculated 'r' is tested as (n-2) degree of freedom with its theoretical value on 5 per cent level of significance.

(e) Chi square test : This test is applied for testing the agreement between observed and expected frequencies when frequencies fall in different classes. This test is applied for enumeration of data, which generally relate to discrete variables. The formula of Chi-square test is as -

$$\chi^2 = \frac{(O_i - E_i)^2}{E_i}$$

Where,

O_i = Observed frequency of ith cell

E_i = Expected frequency of ith cell

The χ^2 cal. < χ^2 tab at á level of significant with $(r-1)(c-1)$ d.f. the Ho that two attributes are independent is accepted.

For testing significance for the case V model of paired comparison method, the test is applied as—

$$\chi^2 = \frac{\Sigma(\theta - \theta')^2}{\theta 21/N}$$

where,

θ = are sin $\sqrt{P}$

N = Number of judgment upon which is based

If χ^2 cal. < χ^2 tab at α level of significance with $(n-1)(n-2)/2$ d.f., the Ho is accepted that statements are tenable.

CHAPTER 5

Findings and Discussion

The empirical results and its discussion have been presented in this chapter. For the purpose of convenience, the presentation has been sub-divided under the following heads :

I. Socio-economic profile of farmwomen

II. Involvement and time utilization of women in farm and home activities through PRA

III. Impact of participation of farm women in PRA technique

IV. Constraints faced by farm women in the adoption of PRA techniques during daily work.

I. Socio-economic Status of Farm Women

Table 5.1. Contribution of respondent according to age

Age group (years)	Frequency	Per cent
25 – 30	26	10.8
30 – 40	121	50.4
40 – 50	73	30.4
50 and above	20	8.4
Total	240	100.00
χ^2	110.768**	P < 0.001

Table 5.1 shows the distribution of farm women according to age. 50.4 per cent farm women belong to 30 to 40 years age group whereas 30.4 per cent women were in 40 to 50 years age group. 10.8 per cent women respondents were in 25 to 30

FINDINGS AND DISCUSSION 51

Village : Tajpur

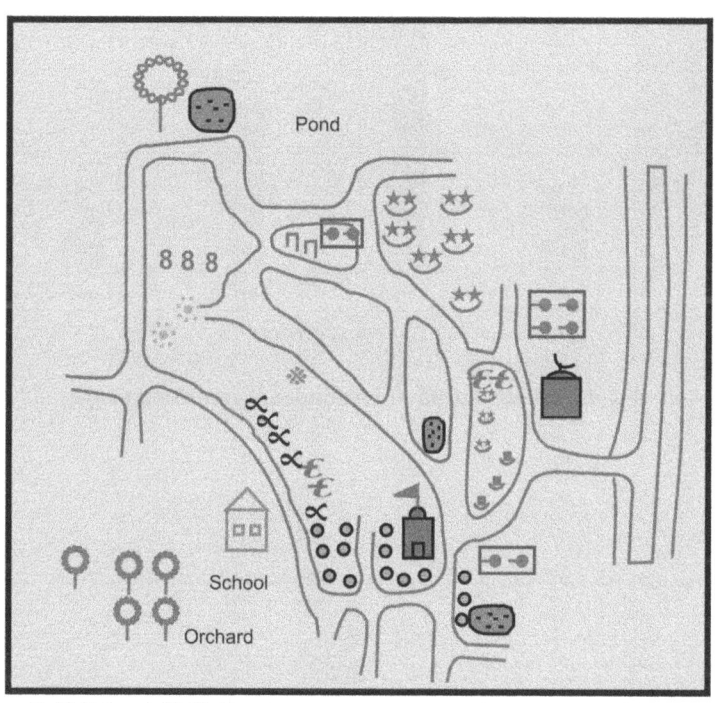

- ○ Yadav
- ※ Saxena
- 🍄 Pathan
- ★★ Mewati
- ∝ Harijan
- ₠ Fakir
- 8 Carpenter
- Π **Barber**
- ⋮⋮ Blacksmith

Social Map 5.1

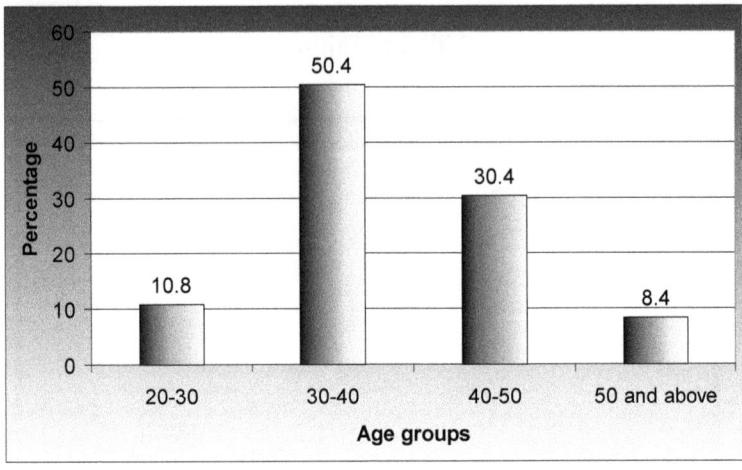

Fig. 5.1. Distribution of respondents according to age.

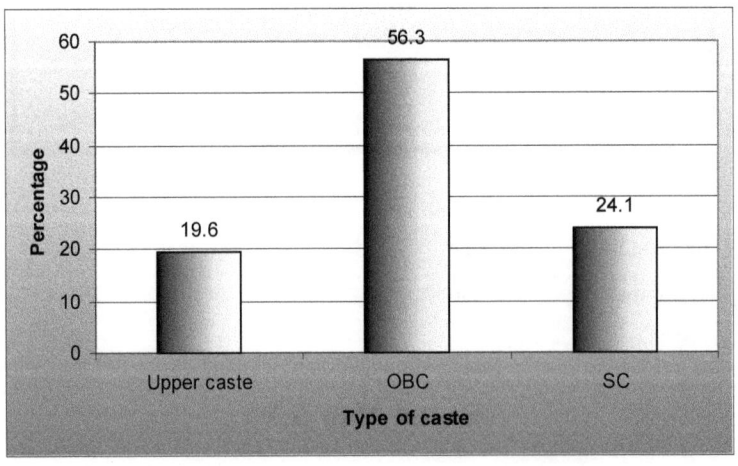

Fig. 5.2. Distribution of respondents on the basis of third caste.

years age groups whereas 8.4 per cent women in 50 and above age group. It means that women when become middle aged they generally get involved in work be it agriculture activity. This is found to be that in Indian culture 30 to 45 years age group women involves herself more in agriculture activity The calculated value of χ^2 (110.768***) was highly significant at 0.1 per cent level of significance.

Table 5.2. Contribution of respondents according to caste

Type of caste	Frequency	Per cent
Upper caste	47	19.6
O.B.C.	135	56.3
SC/ST	58	24.1
Total	240	100.0
χ^2	57.474***	P < 0.001

Table 5.2 indicates that in the study area, 56.3 per cent women respondents were belong to OBC category whereas 24.1 per cent women of SC/ST category and only 19.6 per cent farm women were belonged to upper caste. PRA techniques efficiently treated through relating them with different aspects of village life rather than treating them through direct probing. PRA sessions on different aspects of village life related to caste and religion. The observed value of χ^2 was significant at 0.1 per cent level of significance.

Table 5.3. Distribution of farm women according to education

Education	Frequency	Per cent
Illiterate	28	11.7
Up to primary	74	30.8
Up to secondary	48	20.0
High school	56	23.3
Intermediate and above	34	14.2
Total	240	100.0
χ^2	27.832**	P < 0.01

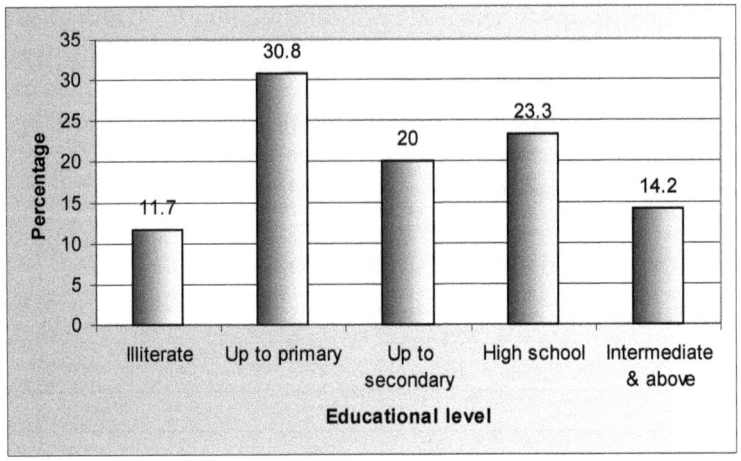

Fig. 5.3. Distribution of respondents according to education level.

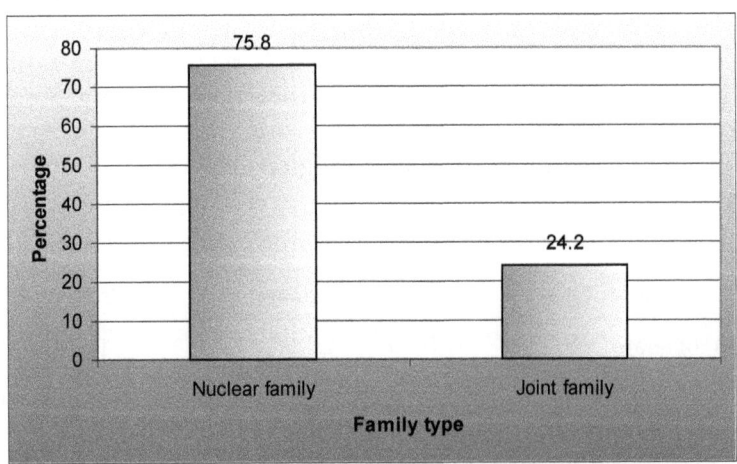

Fig. 5.4. Distribution of farm women according to family size.

The perusal of Table 5.3 reveals that distribution of farm women according to education, 30.8 per cent farm women have educated up to primary level whereas 23.3 per cent women have educated up to high school. 20.0 per cent farm women have educated up to secondary level whereas 11.7 per cent farm women have no education. Participatory rural appraisal (PRA) is a methodology for interacting with villagers, understanding them and learning from them, PRA is seen as most appropriate in terms of collective thinking and action which is geared towards sustainable development and taking new information collectively. The observed value of χ^2 (27.832**) was significant at 1.0 level of significance.

Table 5.4 Distribution of farm women according to type of family

Family type	Frequency	Per cent
Nuclear	182	75.8
Joint	58	24.2
Total	240	100.0
χ^2	64.066***	P < 0.001

The perusal of Table 5.4 reveals that distribution of farm women according to family type, 75.8 per cent farm women were belong to nuclear family whereas 24.2 per cent farm women have belong to joint family system. Now-a-days joint family system is disintegrating into nuclear family system due to environment and male and female are working together. The observed value of χ^2 (64.066***) was significant at 0.1 per cent level of significance.

Table 5.5 Distribution of farm women according to family size

Family type	Frequency	Per cent
Up to 5 members	185	77.1
6 and above members	55	22.9
Total	240	100.0
χ^2	70.416***	P < 0.001

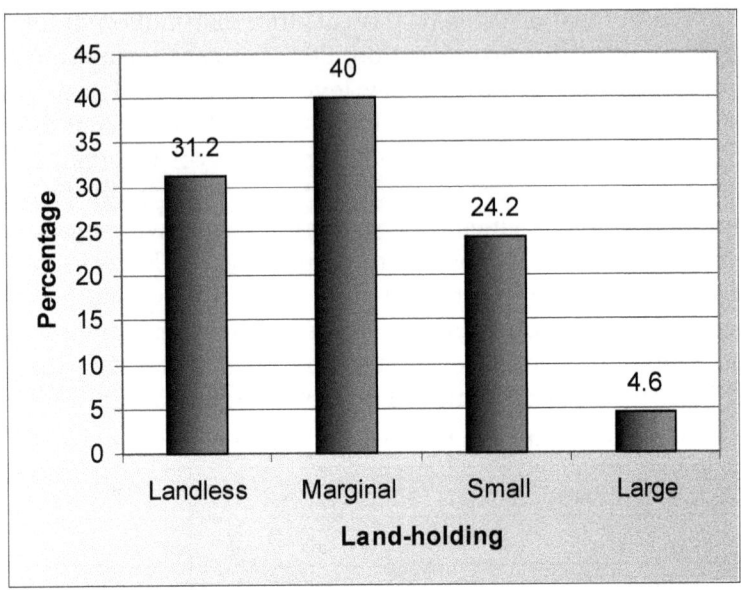

Fig. 5.5. Distribution of farm women according to land-holding.

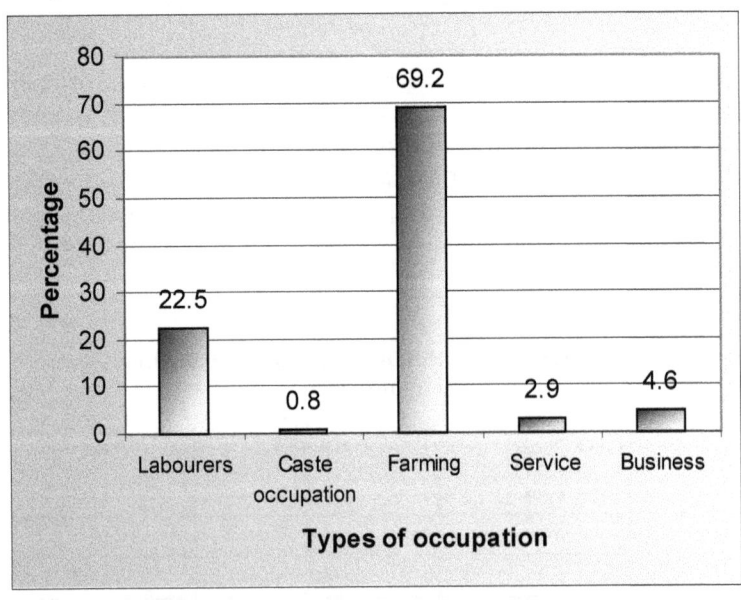

Fig. 5.6. Distribution of farm women according to occupation.

The Table 5.5 indicates that distribution of farm women according to family size, 77.1 per cent farm women have 5 members family size whereas 22.9 per cent women have 6 and above members family size. For monitoring by PRA methods there can be a set of indicators proposed indigenously to guide effective implementation of family size. The calculated value of χ^2 (70.416***) was significant at 0.1 per cent level of significance.

Table 5.6. Distribution of farm women according to monthly income

Monthly income	Frequency	Per cent
Up to Rs. 1500	38	15.9
Rs. 1501 – Rs. 3000	79	32.9
Rs. 3001 – Rs. 4500	62	25.8
Rs. 4501 – Rs. 6000	45	18.7
Rs. 6001 and above	16	6.7
Total	240	100.0
χ^2	47.707**	P < 0.01

Table 5.6 shows that distribution of farm women according to monthly income where 32.9 per cent women have earned Rs. 1501 to Rs. 3000 monthly whereas 25.8 per cent farm women have earned Rs. 3001 to Rs. 4500 monthly. 18.7 per cent women respondents have earned Rs. 4501 to Rs. 6000 monthly whereas 15.9 per cent women earned up to Rs. 1500 monthly. Thus, it may be concluded from the above analysis that majority of respondents belonged to the income group of Rs. 1501 to Rs. 3000.

Table 5.7. Distribution of farm women according to their annual family income

Annual family income	Frequency	Per cent
Up to Rs. 50000	156	65.0
Rs. 50001 and above	84	35.0
Total	240	100.0
χ^2	21.600**	P < 0.01

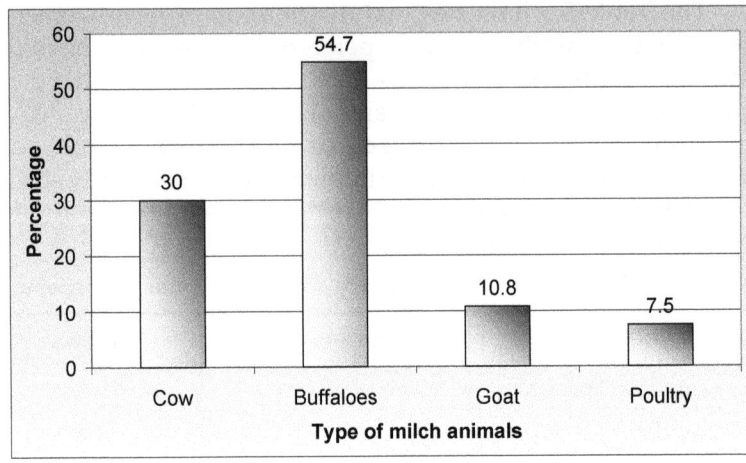

Fig. 5.7. Distribution of farm women according to milch animal.

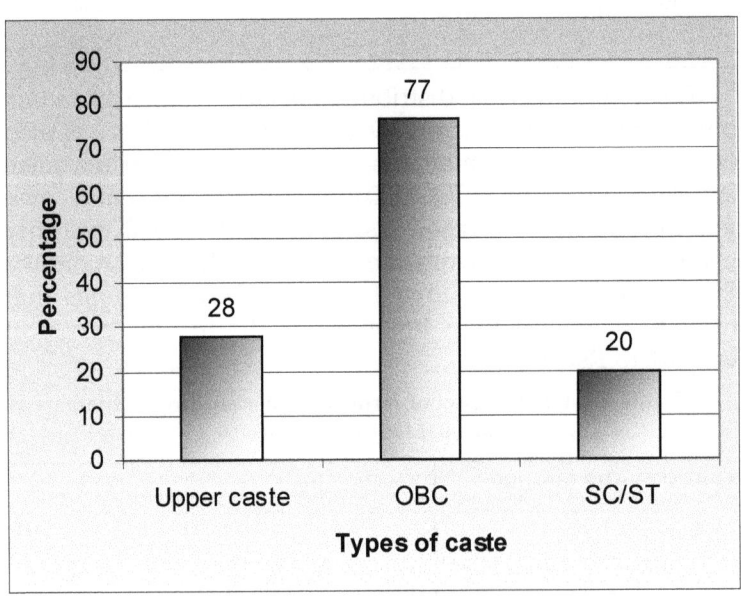

Fig. 5.8. Impact of caste in agriculture activity through PRA.

Table 5.7 reveals that distribution of farm women according to their annual family income, 65.0 per cent farm women have their family annual income up to Rs. 50,000 whereas 35.0 per cent women respondents have annual family income Rs. 50001 and above. The observed value of χ^2 (21.600**) was significant at 1.0 per cent level of significance.

Table 5.8. Distribution of farm women according to land holding

Land holding	Frequency	Per cent
Landless	75	31.2
Marginal	96	40.0
Small	58	24.2
Large	11	4.6
Total	240	100.0
χ^2	65.434***	P < 0.001

The perusal of Table 5.8 reveals that distribution of farm women according to land holding, 40.0 per cent women possessed marginal land whereas 31.2 per cent farm women have no land for farming. 24.2 per cent women have small land while 4.6 per cent farm women have large land whether they have belonged to high economic status. The observed value of χ^2 (65.434***) was significant at 0.1 per cent level of significance.

Table 5.9. Distribution of farm women according to occupation

Occupation	Frequency	Per cent
Labourers	54	22.5
Caste occupation	2	0.8
Farming	166	69.2
Service	7	2.9
Business	11	4.6
Total	240	100.0
χ^2	398.458***	P < 0.001

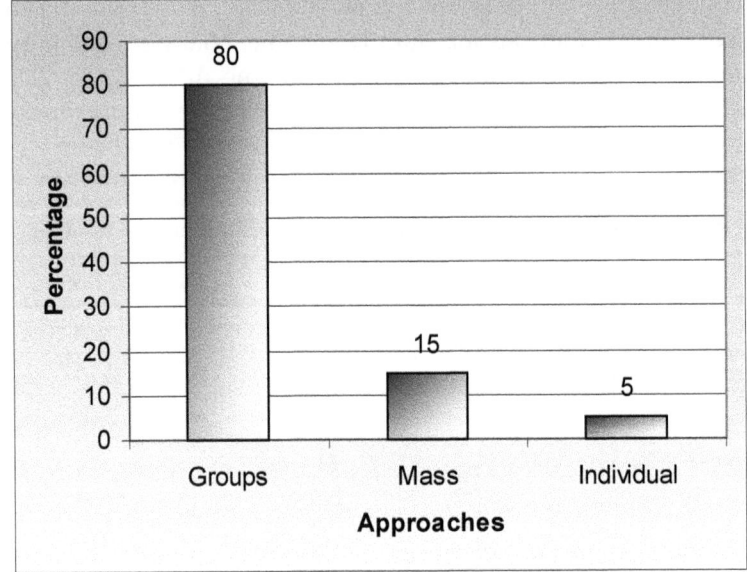

Fig. 5.9. Effect of approaches on PRA.

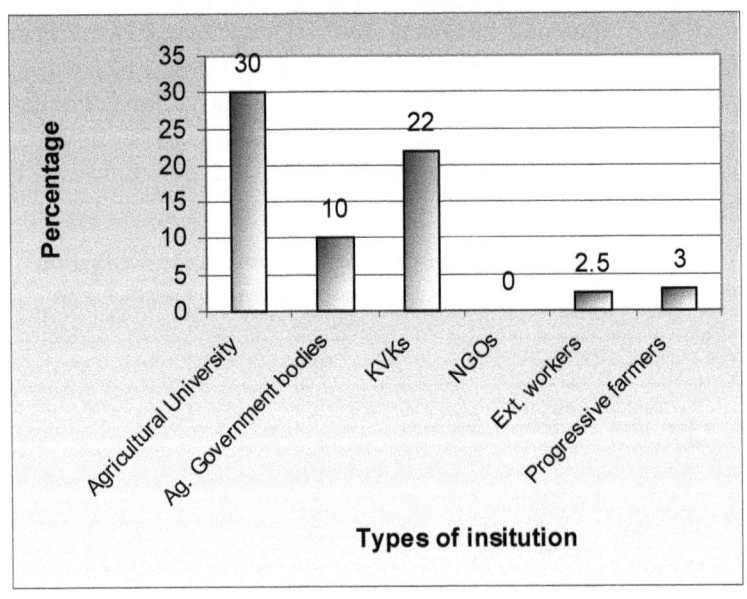

Fig. 5.10. Participation of institution in PRA technique.

Table 5.9 indicates that distribution of farm women according to occupation, 69.2 per cent farm women were doing farming whereas 22.5 per cent farm women were labourers. 4.6 per cent women respondents have engaged in business whereas 2.9 per cent women in service. Women were carrying out farming activity through PRA. The observed value of χ^2 (398.458***) was highly significant at 0.1 per cent level of significance.

Table 5.10 Distribution of farm women according to type of house

Type of house	Frequency	Per cent
Kaccha house	18	7.5
Pucca house	48	20.0
Mixed house	174	72.5
Total	240	100.0
χ^2	171.300***	P < 0.001

Table 5.10 depicts that distribution of women according to type of house, 72.5 per cent women were having mixed house whereas 20.0 per cent women have pucca house. Only 7.5 per cent women have Kaccha house. The observed value of χ^2 (171.300***) was highly significant at 0.1 per cent level of significance.

Table 5.11. Distribution of respondents on the basis of material possession

Material possession	Frequency	Per cent
Up to 5 items	39	16.3
6 to 10 items	165	68.7
11 items and above	36	15.0
Total	240	100.0
χ^2	135.524***	P < 0.001

A perusal of Table 5.11 shows that maximum 68.7 per cent respondents were having 6 to 10 items and 16.3 per cent farm women were having only up to 5 items while remaining 15.0 per cent women were having 11 items and above. The

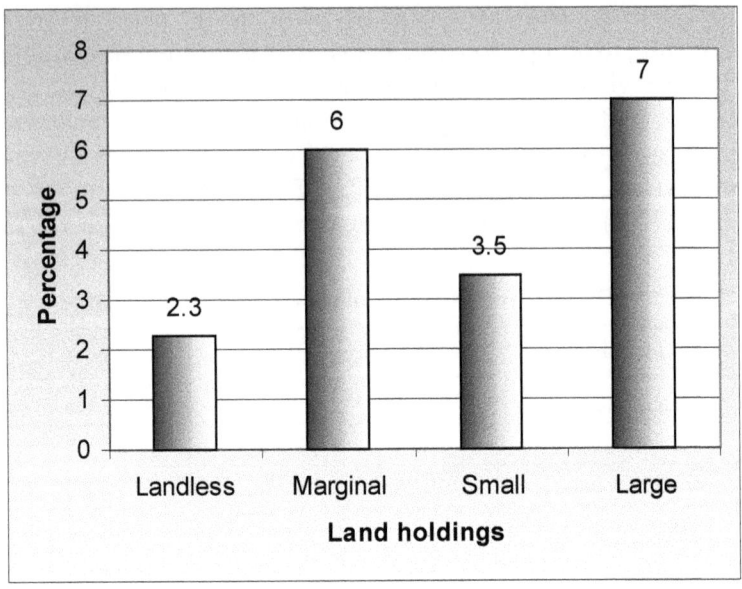

Fig. 5.11. Landholding-wise farming activity through PRA.

calculated value of χ^2 (135.524***) was highly significant at 0.1 per cent level of significance.

Table 5.12 Farm power of the respondent according to land holding

Farm power	Land holding			
	Landless	Marginal	Small	Large
Tractor	-	-	18 (7.5)	33 (13.7)
Thresher	-	3 (1.2)	28 (11.7)	43 (17.9)
Tubewell	-	11 (4.6)	46 (19.2)	60 (25.0)
Generator	-	3 (1.2)	11 (4.6)	22 (9.2)
Winnower	9 (3.7)	21 (8.7)	42 (17.5)	50 (20.8)
Bullocks	-	6 (2.5)	29 (12.1)	32 (13.3)
Khurpi & Phawada	48 (20.0)	42 (17.5)	36 (15.0)	58 (24.02)

The perusal of Table 5.12 reveals that farm power of the women respondents according to land holding, 13.7 per cent large land holding women respondents have tractor whereas 7.5 per cent small land women respondents have tractor. 17.9 per cent women having large land holding have thresher, 25.0 per cent tube well, 20.8 per cent winnower and 13.3 per cent women have bullocks they were large land holding respondents. In small land holding 19.2 per cent women have tube well, 4.6 per cent women have generator, 12.1 per cent women have bullocks and 15.0 per cent women have *Khurpi* and *Phawada*. 20.0 per cent women who were landless have *Khurpi* and *Phawada*.

Table 5.13. Distribution of farm women according to milch animal

Type of house	Frequency	Per cent
Cow	72	30.0
Buffaloes	124	51.7
Goat	26	10.8
Poultry	18	7.5
Total	240	100.0
χ^2	119.334	

Table 5.13 shows the distribution of farm women according to milch animal 51.7 per cent farm women have buffaloes whereas 30.0 per cent farm women have cow for milk business, 10.8 per cent farm women have goat while 7.5 per cent farm women have poultry. On the basis of above analysis it was concluded that the buffalo is the most common milch animal among farmers.

Involvement of Farm Women in Agriculture Activity through PRA Technique Time Line

In time line method, elderly villagers narrate their life histories. Since it is often difficult to remember the exact dates of important changes, a villagers can be facilitated to broadly connect such changes with major events, political regimes and thus, summarise major events and changes that have taken place during his/her life time.

Rural livelihoods are integrally connected with season. Each season has its own problems and the rural people have different strategies for their livelihoods. The seasons bear heavily on the physical conditions which in turn influence their lives. Seasons bring about differences in climatic conditions, in crops grown, in availability of water, food, fuel and fodder which in turn influence the living conditions in rural areas. Seasonal diagramming can lead to comparisons of related aspects of rural livelihoods such as seasonal variations and their linkages with food, employment, work load, disease etc.

Different aspects of rural life can be reflected through seasonal diagramming. A method which reflects the 'seasonal' aspect of rural livelihood is a much better method than a picture presented by some other method such as a questionnaire survey taken at two different points of a year. In the latter case, the 'seasonal' factor can either be neutralized through 'averaging' or conclusions can be drawn on the basis of a partial picture for one season.

Table 5.14 Involvement of farm women in agriculture activity through PRA technique

Agriculture activity	Frequency	Per cent
Time line	85.0	15.0
Seasonal food calendar	86.0	14.0
Seasonal analysis pest disease and crop	85.0	15.0
Land use map	90.0	10.0
Resource map	92.0	8.0
Food protection benefits	88.0	12.0

The perusal of Table 5.14 reveals the involvement of farm women in agriculture activity through PRA technique. 14.0 per cent farm women were involved to make seasonal food calendar through PRA and 15.0 per cent farm women were involved in time line and seasonal analysis pest disease and

Village : Singhpur

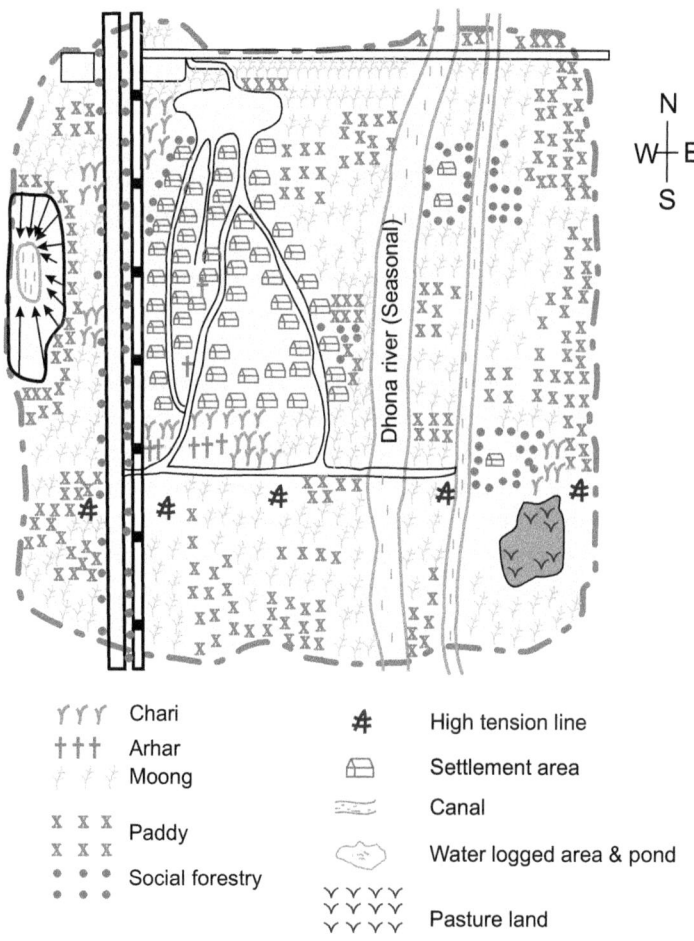

Map 5.2. Land Use

crop respectively. 12.0 per cent farm women have used food protection benefits through PRA whereas 10.0 per cent women respondents have used land use map technique through PRA. Only 8.0 per cent farm women have used resource map through PRA technique in study area, map and history of land, crop and season. The farm map is an ideal tool for knowing the minute details of a farm, its soil conditions, the variations, different crops grown, water management, fertilizer use, yields and ownership. A farm map can help in sequencing of seasonal analysis or livelihood analysis to know more about livelihood patterns of resource poor farmers. On the basis of the village map, the villagers attempted to group the households. They marked the households which were at the lowest strata of poverty according to their perceptions. These included the widowed households which had single widows as heads of households and were maintaining livelihoods with practically no assets, no regular source of income and not enough to eat throughout the year. Others in this group included agricultural labourers having neither any land, nor any regular source of income or food. 32.0 per cent farm women were used harvesting technique in general method through traditional, winnowing technique and weeding technique through traditional method.

Food calendar is a specific use of seasonal diagramming. Seasonal variations in food availability is an integral part of rural life and the PRA method of food calendar can illustrate food availability in different seasons. Both the quantum and the kind of food availability over different seasons or months can be shown through a food calendar.

Table 5.15 shows the involvement of farm women in agricultural activities. According to season (*Rabi, Kharif,* and *Zaid*) in time line, elderly narrate their life histories, since it is often difficult to remember the exact dates of important changes, a villager can be facilitated to broadly connect such changes with major events and changes that have taken place during her life time, yield, population, livestock population, number of trees, area under cultivation, rainfall, time and

FINDINGS AND DISCUSSION 67

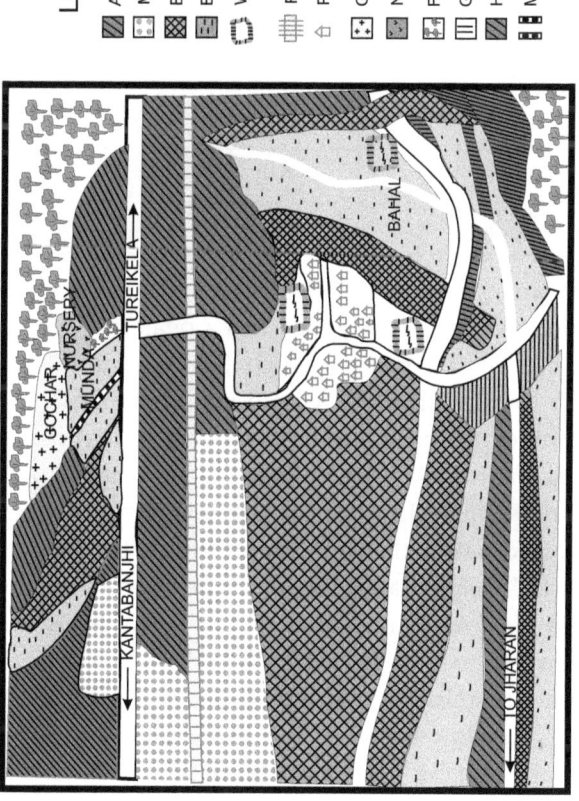

Resource Map 5.3. Land Use

distance to collect fuel wood and fodder etc. one can directly or indirectly see the increase or decrease of hardship in poor people's lives.

Table 5.15. Involvement of farm women in agricultural activities according to season

Agricultural activity	Rabi	Kharif	Zaid
Time line	5.0	6.0	4.0
Seasonal food calendar	4.0	8.0	2.0
Seasonal analysis pest diseases and crop	7.0	6.0	2.0
Land use map	4.0	3.0	3.0
Resource map	4.0	3.0	1.0
Food protection benefits	6.0	4.0	2.0

Farm women have engaged in seasonal food growing in terms of food availability, rice reaches a peak in *'Magh'* (mid January to mid February) after which it declines until *'Chaitra'* (mid March to mid April) to remain stationary until *'Aswin'* (mid September to mid October) whereas wheat reaches a peak in *'Baisakh'* (mid April to mid May) after which it declines until *'Jyaistha'* (mid May to mid June). Eating of potatoes follows approximately the same trend as rice for the months of *'Magh'* and *'Phalgun'* and then declines sharply during the period from *'Chaitra'* (Mid March to mid April) to *'Agrahyan'* (mid November to mid December) and picks up again in *'Poush'* (mid December to mid January). Intake of pulses as a food item is very low in the month of *'Baisakh'* and is higher in the months of *'Sawan'*, *'Agrahyan'* and *'Poush'*. Rural women in general have more knowledge than rural men in depicting the variety of food which they generally go and collect from different sources like from ponds, river beds, forests, wild trees in the village and nearby areas. The village farm women try to hedge against low food availability. The farm women can be empowered to collaborate in such projects like agroforestry can include seasonal plants whose flower, fruits, leaves, vegetables, roots and stems can be used to supplement the food intake of the villagers. Farm women are generally busy throughout the day in their households. They explained their work relating to both households and outside their households and listed their schedule of different activities which they perform.

Seasonal analysis helps in understanding seasonal cyclic variations in the selected parameters such as rainfall, temperature, humidity, cropping systems, crop rotations, labour availability, fodder availability, disease occurrence etc. Seasonal analysis may be done through drawing of seasonal diagrams through PRA. The member are asked to draw the diagram for a given year preferably starting from first month to *Kharif* season i.e. July and up to month of June. For instance, duration of crops, occurrence of crop pests and diseases, occurrence of livestock diseases and fodder availability in a calendar year.

The resource map of a village can show different kinds of natural resources. In a resource map, the villagers depict different kinds of rivers, ponds, trees, crop, animal species and the land utilization pattern. Land for crop like arhar, moong, paddy, social forestry, canal, waterlogged area and pond, pasture land, high tension line and settlement area. Participatory resource map of land like Panchayat Ghar, shop, store, temple, irrigated area, unirrigated area, reserve forest and fruit trees. The rural farm women perform activities range from child rearing to household activities and farm operations. The rural women play a crucial role in most rural activities and their participation can be solicited to learn about their knowledge gained in the process of performing such activities.

Village – Pali

Items \ Month	No. of stoned Rice	No. of stoned Potato	No. of stoned Pulse	Vegetables	Fruits	Food from other source	Others from wild
MAGH (mid-Jan to mid-Feb)	15	13	3	Cabbage			Wild borums wild rabbits
PHALGUN (mid-Feb to mid-March)	9	11	2	Spinach			Neem leaves
CHITRA (mid-March to mid-April)	4	4	2	Pumpkin		Fish & wild water plants	
BAISAKH (mid-April to mid-May)	4	3	1	Puileaves (Herbs)	*Mango *Jack fruit	Fish & Water plants	
JYAISTHA (mid-May to mid-June)	4	4	2	'Lota' leaves (Herbs)	*Mango *Jack fruit	Fish & Wild Water plants	
ASHAR (mid-June to mid-July)	4	3	3	'Jhinge'			
SRAVAN (mid-July to mid-Aug)	4	4	5	Papaya			
BHADRA (mid-Aug. to mid-Sept.)	4	3	3	Green Banana		Fish and Snails	
AHWIN (Mid-Sept. to mid-Oct.)	4	3	2				
KARTICK (mid-Oct. to mid-Nov.)	2	4	3	Raddish Leaves			
AGRAHAYAN (mid Nov. to mid-Dec.)	2	4	5	Tomato			
POUSH (mid-Dec. to mid-Jan.)	2	9	6	Brinjal			Wild Rabbits

Note: The number specified under rice, potato and pulses represents the no. of stones shown by villagers,
*shown fruits of trees growing nearby.
Women village analysis Smt. Suneeta, Rama, Savita Devi.

Map 5.4. Seasonal Food Calendar

FINDINGS AND DISCUSSION

Table 5.16. Involvement of farm women in agricultural activities according to season

Agricultural activity	Time utilization (hrs/day)		
	Rabi	Kharif	Zaid
Time line	3 (12.5)	2 (8.3)	1 (4.2)
Seasonal food calendar	2 (8.3)	1½ (6.3)	½ (2.1)
Seasonal analysis pest disease and crop	1½ (6.3)	1 (4.2)	½ (2.1)
Land use map	1½ (6.3)	1½ (6.3)	½ (2.1)
Resource map	1½ (6.3)	1 (4.2)	½ (2.1)
Food protection benefits	2 (8.3)	1½ (6.3)	½ (2.1)

(Figures in parentheses denotes per cent values)

Table 5.16 shows the time utilization of farm women according to PRA. In *Rabi* season farm women spent her time (12.5%) in time line technique through PRA, 8.3 per cent time in seasonal food calendar, 6.3 per cent time in seasonal analysis pest diseases and crop, 6.3 per cent in land use map and resource map respectively. In *Kharif* season farm women spent her time 8.3 per cent in time line, 6.3 per cent time in seasonal food calendar, land use map and food protection benefits respectively. In *Zaid* season farm women spent her time 4.2 per cent in time line and 2.1 per cent time in other agricultural activities through PRA. Rural livelihoods are integrally connected with seasonality. Each season has its own problems and the rural farm women have different strategies for their livelihoods. A method livelihood is a much better method such as a questionnaire survey taken at three seasons (*Rabi, Kharif* and *Zaid*). Rural farm women are generally busy throughout the day mostly in their households but 6 to 7 hours time spent in agriculture activity. A large number of them also work outside on their own with the male members of their households besides having exclusive responsibility of running households.

72 PARTICIPATORY RURAL APP. TECH. FOR FARM WOMEN

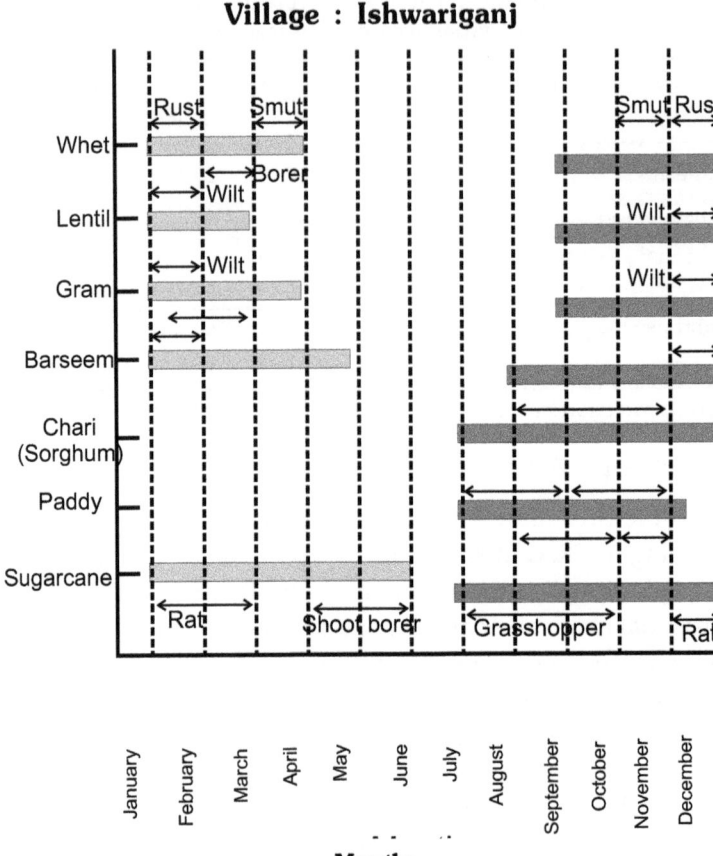

Map 5.5. Seasonal Analysis of Pests and Diseases in Crops.

Table 5.17. Involvement of farm women in dairy activities through PRA technique

Dairy activity	Traditional	Through PRA technique
Use in farm operation	65.0	35.0
Milk yield	55.0	45.0
Meat production	80.0	20.0
Manure		
(i) Compost	70.0	30.0
(ii) Cow dung	95.0	5.0
(iii) Gobar gas plant	65.0	35.0
For drafting	55.0	45.0
For sale purpose	75.0	25.0
Additional income by milk product	35.0	65.0

Table 5.17 reveals the involvement of women in animal husbandry practices through PRA technique. In animal husbandry activity 65.0 per cent women were used traditional method in farm operation whereas 55.0 per cent women respondents used milk yield by traditionally. In case of manure like compost and gobar gas plant mostly farm women have used through PRA technique. 45.0 per cent women respondents have used drafting through PRA technique. 65.0 per cent women respondents were used methods through PRA for sale purpose of dairy products.

Table 5.18 reveals the time utilization pattern of farm women in dairy activity through PRA, maximum time spent of farm women in milk yield 8.3 per cent in winter and summer. Farm women spent her 4.2 per cent time in meat production in winter and summer season. In compost and cow dung manure, farm women spent her 6.2 per cent time in

Village : Gangapur

Kinds of Animal / Criteria	Cattle	Buffalo	Goat	Poultry
Use in farm operations	●●● ●●●	●●● ●●	●	—
Milk yield	—	● ●●	●● ●●	—
Meat production	—	—	●● ●●	●● ●●
For manure	● ●	●● ●●	●● ●●	●● ●●
For eggs	—	—	—	● ●
For drafting	●● ●● ●	●●● ●●	—	—
Productive age duration	●● ● ●	●●● ●●●	●	●
Additional income	● ●	●● ●●	●	● ●
Rank	II	I	IV	III

Map 5.6. Matrix Ranking of Livestock and Poultry Production

winter and summer season while in rainy season she spent her less time in these activities. For drafting in all season and they spent in same manner, 6.2 per cent time in summer season for additional income by milk product. In all animal husbandry activities mostly worked out by women and minimum involvement of women in animal sale, making models and animal grazing. Time schedule through PRA technique for women so that they adopt modern technology and reduce work load by provide training of drudgery reducing equipment, they can improve work efficiency and reduce drudgery. For sale purpose farm women spent 1 hour time in winter and summer season through PRA technique.

Table 5.18. Time utilization pattern of farm women in dairy activity through PRA

Dairy activity	Time utilization (hrs/day)		
	Rabi	Kharif	Zaid
Use in farm operations	1½ (6.2)	1½ (6.2)	1 (4.2)
Milk yield	2 (8.3)	2 (8.3)	2 (8.3)
Meat production	1 (4.2)	1 (4.2)	½ (2.1)
Manure			
(i) Compost	1½ (6.2)	1½ (6.2)	½ (2.1)
(ii) Cow dung	1½ (6.2)	1½ (6.2)	½ (2.1)
(iii) Gobar gas plant	1 (4.2)	1 (4.2)	1 (4.2)
For drafting	½ (2.1)	½ (2.1)	½ (2.1)
For sale purpose	1 (4.2)	1 (4.2)	½ (2.1)
Additional income by milk product	1 (4.2)	1½ (6.2)	½ (2.1)

(Figures in parentheses denotes per cent values)

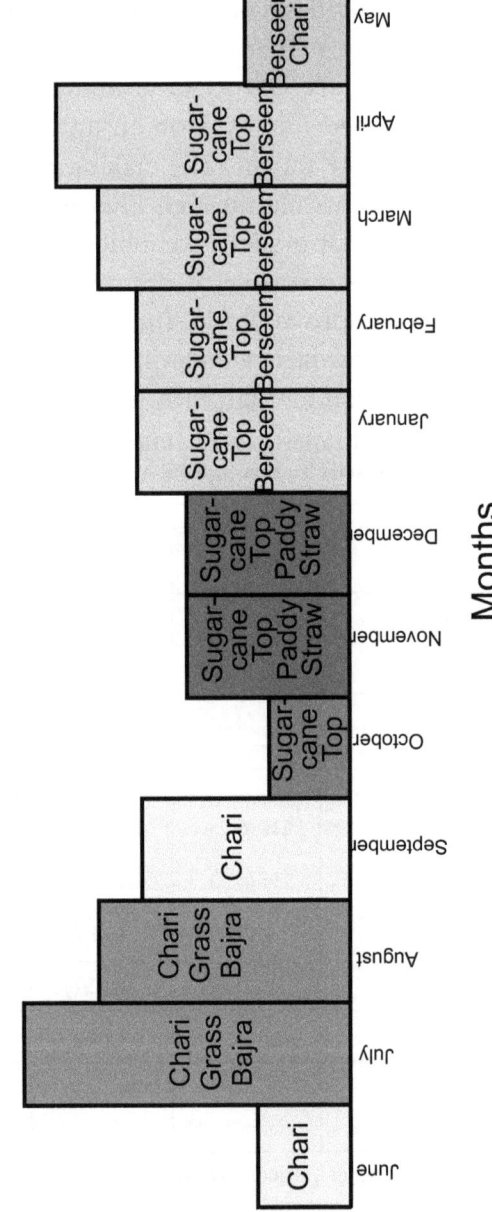

Map 5.7. Green Fodder Availability

Involvement of Women in Household Activities Through PRA Technique

Rural women are generally busy throughout the day mostly in their households. A large number of them also work outside on their own or share outside work with the male members of their households besides having exclusive responsibility of running households. Much of such work is of a routine nature and is repetitive. Rural women generally have a busy schedule to cope up with day to day responsibility. As a result, they seldom find much time for themselves either to relax or to do something different. In a PRA session in village Banstaol, district Tangail, Bangladesh, a group of women were approached in order to learn about their daily routine activities. They narrated their daily work schedule as described below.

At first, it was a session of rapport building with the women in the village of Banstaol. Later the PRA team enquired about the role of women in farm activities. On this aspect, the women replied that they were actively involved in growing of brinjals and bananas as well as other food crops. Preliminary activities in paddy fields were also done by them. However, they did not practice cultivation. They were basically engaged in supplementary activities in the fields. They explained their work relating to both households and outside their households and listed their schedule of different activities which they perform.

Table 5.19 shows the involvement of farm women in household activities through PRA technique. 75.0 per cent farm women have used traditionally technique for sweeping and cleaning house whereas 70.0 per cent farm women have traditionally cleaning utensils. 92.0 per cent farm women traditionally adopted method for fetching water for cooking and 70.0 per cent farm women were preparing food traditionally. Through PRA 35.0 per cent, 45.0 per cent farm women were making weaving mats and weaving fences from bamboo sticks, respectively. Community empowerment would enhance their level of involvement in the development process. It can liberate the energy of the community to work, innovate and diversify its livelihood base. Community involvement is an exercise in 'learning by doing' for the community and development agencies and depends on the gains perceived through such action. Community empowerment can play a powerful role in creating a sustainable system of agriculture, by use of local resources, lower dependence on external inputs and adopt agro-ecological technologies which are environment friendly.

Table 5.19. Involvement of women in household activities through PRA technique

Household activities	Traditional	Through PRA technique
Sweeping and cleaning house	75.0	25.0
Cleaning utensils	70.0	30.0
Giving fodder to cattle and goats	70.0	30.0
Fetching water for cooking	92.0	8.0
Preparing food	70.0	30.0
Child rearing	75.0	25.0
Weaving mats	65.0	35.0
Weaving fences from bamboo sticks	55.0	45.0

Daily routine diagrams reflect the kind of activities which one does on a daily basis. It cannot only show the time spent in different activities but also the size of the work involved. For instance, women spend different hours of day in activities like feeding children, cooking, fetching water, grazing livestock, collecting firewood and fuel wood. It is possible to identify general patterns from daily patterns. The general patterns of different groups can then be compared. Such daily routines can also be depicted on a seasonal basis in order to identify constraints and workloads of different groups related to different activities.

FINDINGS AND DISCUSSION 79

Village : Tilsehri

AM	Hour	PM	Legend
Sleeping	1	Resting	Sleeping
Sleeping	2	Sweeping	Sweeping
Sleeping	3	Harvesting / Weeding	Praying
Sleeping	4	Cooking	Cooking
Praying	5	Cooking	Lifting water
Marketing items	6	Cooking	Going to school
Sweeping / Going to school	7	Eating	Weeding Planting
Lifting water / Fetching firewood	8	Praying	Marketing
Sweeping / Cooking	9	Resting	Washing plate
Sweeping	10	Sleeping	Resting
Sweeping	11	Sleeping	Harvesting
Cooking	12	Sleeping	Fetching firewood
			Returning from farm
			Eating

Map 5.8. Daily Activity Schedule of Women

Time

Table 5.20 Time utilization pattern of women in animal husbandry practices through PRA according to income group
(hrs per day per head)

Sl. No.	Farm power	Land holding			
		Landless	Marginal	Small	Large
1.	Sweeping and cleaning house	1.5 (6.2)	1.5 (6.2)	2 (8.3)	1 (4.2)
2.	Cleaning utensils	2 (8.3)	1.5 (6.2)	1 (4.2)	-
3.	Giving fodder to cattle and goats	1 (4.2)	1 (4.2)	-	-
4.	Fetching water for cooking	1 (4.2)	1 (4.2)	1 (4.2)	-
5.	Preparing food for household	2 (8.3)	1.5 (6.2)	1.5 (6.2)	2 (8.3)
6.	Child rearing	1 (4.2)	1 (4.2)	1.5 (6.2)	2 (8.3)
7.	Weave mats	-	1 (4.2)	1 (4.2)	1 (4.2)
8.	Weave fences from bamboo & sticks				

Table 5.20 reveals the time utilization of farm women in household activities. Landless women respondents spent her 6.2 per cent time in sweeping and cleaning house, 8.3 per cent time in cleaning utensils, 4.2 per cent time giving fodder to cattle and goats, fetching water for cooking and child rearing. Apart from work in agriculture activities, dairy activity the rural farm women also have a busy schedule of household work. Gender discrimination is practiced widely against women in most countries of the world, one aspect of gender discrimination is often found in food intake inside households. Rural farm women generally have a busy schedule to cope up with day to day responsibility, they seldom find much time for themselves either to relax or to do something different. Marginal land owner women spent more time in sweeping and cleaning house, cleaning utensils and preparing food for

FINDINGS AND DISCUSSION

Village : Phuphuwar

SEASONAL HEALTH CALENDER
Seasonality with Scoring

MONTHS / DISEASES	JAN	FEB	MAR	APR	MAY	JUN	JUL	AUG	SEP	OCT	NOV	DEC
Fever				••	•	•					••••• ••••	••
Cold & Whooping cough	••										•••• ••••	•••
Headache	•••• ••••			•••• ••••			•••	•••	•••	•••• ••••	•••• ••••	•••• ••••
Diarrhoea				•••• ••••	•••		••		•	•••• ••••		
Measles				•••• ••••	••••	••						
Jaundice	•••	•••		•••								
Vomiting	•	•••		•	•••				•••• ••••	•••• ••••		
Scabies		••	•••	•••• ••••	•••• ••••		••	••	•••	•••		
Tetanus									•	•••• ••••	•••• ••••	•••
MONTHS	JAN	FEB	MAR	APR	MAY	JUN	JUL	AUG	SEP	OCT	NOV	DEC

Map 5.9.

household members. Small and large land owner women respondents spent her much time in cooking food, child rearing, weaving mats and weaving fences from bamboo sticks. In a PRA technique in village a group of women were approached in order to learn about their daily routine of activities. They were basically engaged in supplementary activities in the fields.

Table 5.21. Involvement and time utilization of farm women in other activities

Other activities	Involvement		Time utilization (hrs/day)
	Frequency	Per cent	
Agricultural activities			
Commercial crop	122	50.8	3.0
Floriculture	72	30.0	1.0
Interculture crop	48	20.0	1.5
Forestry	12	5.0	1.0
Dairy activities			
Selling milk	180	75.0	3.0
Selling milk product	72	30.0	1.5
Selling cow dung compost	192	80.0	3.0
Selling animals	72	30.0	1.0
Household activities			
Poultry	72	30.0	1.0
Goatry	144	60.0	1.5
Bee keeping	192	80.0	2.0
Piggery	24	10.0	1.0
Other income generating household activity	48	20.0	1.5

Table 5.21 reveals the involvement and time utilization of farm women in three areas through PRA farm women have involved 50.8 per cent in commercial crop whereas 30.0 per

FINDINGS AND DISCUSSION 83

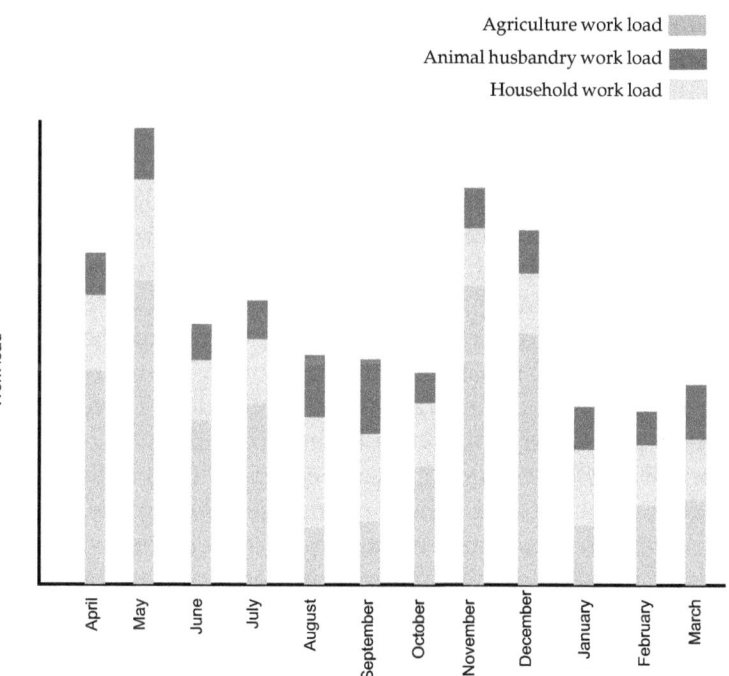

Map 5.10. Seasonal analysis of workload of farm women

cent involved in floriculture and scoring reveal priorities and preferences. Rural farm women have integrally connected with season. Each season has its own problems and the farm women have different strategies for their livelihoods. The seasons bear heavily on the physical conditions which in turn influence their lives. Seasons bring about differences in climatic conditions, in crops grown, in availability of water, food, fuel and fodder which in turn influence the living conditions in rural areas. In dairy activity rural farm women have involved 80.0 per cent in selling cow dung compost and 75.0 per cent in selling milk, whereas 30.0 per cent farm women were involved in selling milk product. Rural women have reluctance to participate for many reasons, they are often busy in their households and other places of work and may not be able to find enough time for outside other activities. The women were the ones who collected fuel wood and fodder from nearby forests and water from wells located near the village. Rural women mostly engaged in bee keeping (80.0 %) followed by goatry (60.0 %) and other income generating household activities. The rural farm women perform activities which are mostly household child rearing and farm operations. Many of such activities are directly visible and tangible in terms of economic gains.

In other agricultural activities farm women spent her time three and half hours per day in interculture crop followed by 1.5 hrs in commercial crop and forestry, respectively. In dairy activity farm women spent her time 3.0 hrs in selling milk product followed by 1.5 hrs in selling milk per day. In household activities farm women spent her time 1.0 hrs in poultry and other income generating household activity while 1.5 hrs in goatry and farm women have spent her time 2.0 hrs/day in bee keeping activity.

Table 5.22 shows per cent work load of farm women in agriculture, dairy and household according to summer, rainy and winter, cropping system, fuel availability, fodder availability. Landless farm women spent maximum per cent time in agriculture activity in summer, rainy and winter

Table 5.22. Workload of farm women according to season in agriculture and household activity

Activity	Landless			Marginal			Small			Large		
	Summer	Rainy	Winter	Summer	Rainy	Winter	Summer	Rainy	Winter	Summer	Rainy	Winter
Agriculture Work	70.0	50.0	65.0	60.0	40.0	40.0	50.0	40.0	30.0	40.0	25.0	20.0
Dairy work	15.0	30.0	15.0	25.0	30.0	25.0	30.0	30.0	30.0	20.0	20.0	20.0
Household	15.0	20.0	20.0	15.0	30.0	35.0	20.0	30.0	40.0	40.0	55.0	60.0

86 PARTICIPATORY RURAL APP. TECH. FOR FARM WOMEN

Village : Pali

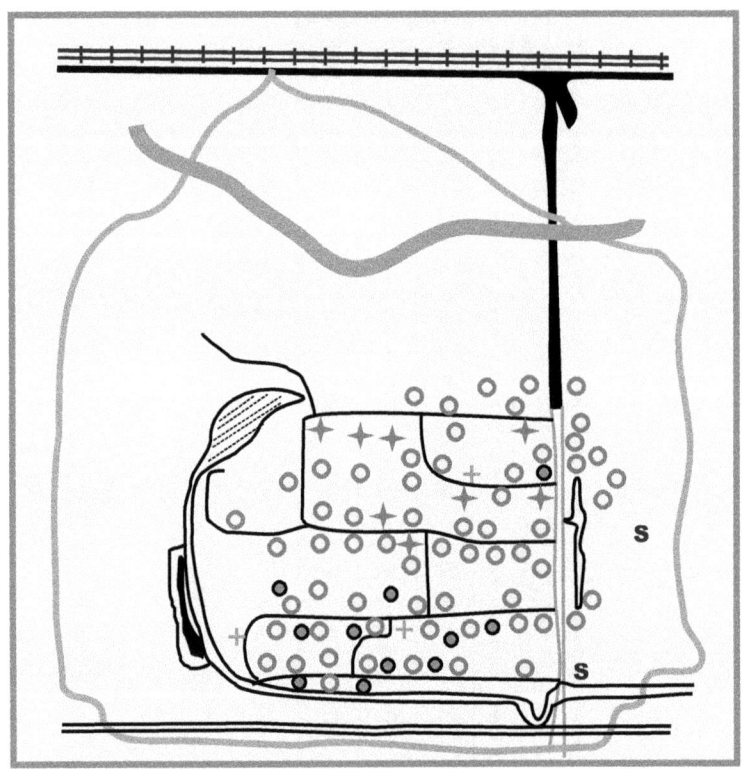

Legend:
+ Farming + Dairy (Mainly cross bred)
○ Farming + Dairy (Mainly buffalo & local breeds)
+ Farming + Dairy + Service
S Piggery + Labour
● Farming + Labour

Map 5.11. Enterprise Map

season. Marginal farm women spend her time in agriculture as well as dairy activity. Small and large land owner farm women have engaged in household activity and dairy activity.

Table 5.23. Month-wise distribution of workload in agriculture, dairy and household activities

Months	Agriculture (hrs/day)	Dairy (hrs/day)	Household (hrs/day)
April	7.0	2.0	4.5
May	7.5	2.0	4.0
June	6.0	2.5	5.0
July	5.0	1.5	6.0
August	6.0	1.0	6.3
September	6.5	2.0	5.0
October	7.0	2.0	5.0
November	6.5	1.5	6.0
December	6.5	2.0	7.0
January	6.0	2.0	8.0
February	6.5	2.0	7.5
March	7.0	2.0	6.0

Table 5.23 shows month wise distribution of load of farm women in agriculture, dairy and household activities. Farm women spent 7 hrs in April in agriculture activity, 7.5 hrs in May, 6.0 hrs in June, 5.0 hrs in July, 6.0 hrs in August and 7.0 hrs in March. Thus in harvesting and sowing time of crop in *Rabi* and *Kharif* season farm women spent her maximum time. In rainy season like July and August farm women have spent her less time in dairy activity because they were not making cow-dung cake, manure and grazing animals. Farm women spent her 2 hrs per day in dairy activity in the month of December, January, February and March. In household activities farm women spent her time average 6.0 hrs per day in various practices cleaning, washing, preparing food and child-rearing. Farm women found time from agriculture

activity she spent that in household activity. The tool of PRA is used for depicting quantitative changes over a time in different aspects of rural farm women life.

Table 5.24. Time utilization of farm women according to household activities

Household activity	Agriculture activity			
	Landless	Marginal	Small	Large
Work in home	3 (12.5)	3 (12.5)	4 (16.7)	5 (20.8)
Income generation	5 (20.8)	4 (16.7)	3 (12.5)	2 (8.3)
Time for self	1 (4.2)	2 (8.3)	2 (8.3)	2 (8.3)

(Figures in parentheses denotes per cent values)

Table 5.24 shows the daily routine work of the farm women spend different hours per day in activities like feeding children, cooking, fetching water, grazing livestock, collecting firewood and fuel wood. It is possible to identify general patterns from daily patterns. Daily routines can also be depicted on a seasonal basis in order to identify constraints and workloads of different groups related to different activities. Landless women have given maximum time to farming while marginal land owner women have given in farming and home activities. Small land and large land owner women spend time in home and time for self. Landless farm women were generally expand more her time in income generating household activities and 12.5 per cent time in work home. Marginal land holding farm women were spent her time (16.7 %) in income generating household activities while small land holding farm women were spent her time (16.7 %) in work home like fetching water, preparing food, feeding child and cleaning utensils. Large land holding farm women respondents have spent her time (20.8 %) in home work and 8.3 per cent time in income generating activity and time for self respectively.

Table 5.25 reveals the estimates of return from production to compare traditional and PRA, traditional to PRA agriculture

Table 5.25. Estimates of return from production to compare traditional and PRA

Estimates of return from various activities	Traditional		Through PRA		Per cent increase (Rs.)
	Production	Price (Rs.)	Production	Price (Rs.)	
Agriculture crop					
(a) Paddy	2 q	400.00	3 q	600.00	50.0
(b) Wheat	2 q	200.00	2 ½ q	250.00	25.0
(c) Maize	1½ q	375.00	2 q	500.00	33.3
(d) Gram	1½ q	600.00	2 q	800.00	33.3
(e) Jowar	1½ q	450.00	2 q	600.00	33.3
(f) Sarson	2 q	1000	2½ q	1500.00	50.0
Dairy return					
(a) Milk selling (per day)	15 litre	180.00	20 litres	240.00	33.3
(b) Cow dung (per day)	100 dung	25.00	100 dung	25.00	-
(c) Milk products (per day)	20 kg	200.00	25 kg	250.00	25.0
Household return					
(a) Poultry					
(b) Packaging material	200 packet	25.00	250 packet	31.00	24.0
(c) Weaving bags and basket	50 bags	1500.00	75 bags	2250.00	50.0

crop were given more profit like Rs. 200/ha in paddy, Rs. 50/ha in wheat, Rs. 125/ha in maize, Rs. 75/ha in jowar and Rs. 250/ha in Sarson. Most farm women were not proper literate and some were illiterate, they arrived at estimates of earnings from crops grown, dairy activities and household activities. In dairy return the PRA techniques are more useful than traditional in milk selling which increases the milk production and selling of milk products. Depletion and degradation of forests are those of indigenous activities to which farm women have an integral relationship and they also bear the brunt with its rapid degradation and disappearance. The process of participation was such that farm women of different social status and religion were involved. Resource mapping was used for identification and location of natural resource and to generate discussions on different crop yield and earning methods of household and dairy activities.

Table 5.26. Impact of caste in agriculture activity through PRA

Caste	Agriculture activity	
	Traditional	PRA
Upper caste	19 (7.9)	28 (11.7)
OBC	58 (24.2)	77 (32.1)
SC/ST	38 (15.8)	20 (8.3)
χ^2	9.584*	$P < 0.05$

(Figures in parentheses denotes per cent values)

A perusal of Table 5.26 shows the caste wise impact through PRA in agriculture activity. It is observed that 32.1 per cent women respondents belong to OBC category were involved in agricultural activity through PRA whereas 8.3 per cent SC/ST women respondents were involved in agricultural activity through PRA. The observed value of χ^2 (9.584*) was significant at 5 per cent level of significance in case of upper caste and SC/ST women, does agricultural activities through PRA.

Table 5.27. Impact of family type of farm women in agriculture activity through PRA.

Family type	Agriculture activity	
	Traditional	PRA
Nuclear	91 (37.9)	91 (37.9)
Joint	24 (10.0)	34 (14.2)
χ^2	1.310	$P > 0.05$

(Figures in parentheses denotes per cent values)

A perusal of Table 5.27 reveals that family type impact through PRA in agriculture activity. It is revealed that maximum (37.9%) women respondents belong to nuclear family system involved in agriculture activity through PRA whereas, 14.2 per cent rural respondents were belong to joint family system involved in agriculture activity through PRA. The observed value of χ^2 1.310 was non-significant at 5 per cent level of significance at 5 degrees of freedom.

Table 5.28. Impact in agriculture activity through education of farm women

Education	Agriculture activity	
	Traditional	PRA
Illiterate	22 (9.2)	6 (2.5)
Primary	40 (16.7)	34 (14.2)
Secondary	24 (10.0)	24 (10.0)
High school	20 (8.3)	36 (15.0)
Intermediate & above	9 (3.7)	25 (10.4)
χ^2	21.351*	P < 0.05

(Figures in parentheses denotes per cent values)

It is revealed from Table 5.28 that 14.2 per cent women respondents educated up to primary level involved in agriculture activity through PRA whereas 2.5 per cent illiterate women respondents involve herself in agriculture activity through PRA. 10.0 per cent women respondents educated up to secondary level were involved in agriculture activity through PRA and 15.0 per cent women respondents educated up to high school level were involved in agriculture activity through PRA. The observed value of χ^2 (21.351*) significant at 5 per cent level of significance.

A perusal of Table 5.29 reveals that in land holding impact through PRA in agriculture activity, 14.6, 9.6 and 2.9 per cent women respondents having small land holding, landless and large land holding respectively imparts agricultural activities through PRA. The observed value of χ^2 (20.132**) was significant at 1 per cent level of significance.

Table 5.29. Landholding-wise farming activity through PRA

Land holding	Agriculture activity	
	Traditional	PRA
Landless	52 (21.7)	23 (9.6)
Marginal	36 (15.0)	60 (25.0)
Small	23 (9.6)	35 (14.6)
Large	4 (1.7)	7 (2.9)
χ^2	20.132**	P < 0.01

(Figures in parentheses denotes per cent values)

Table 5.30. Impact of age group in dairy activity of farm women

Age-group (years)	Dairy activity	
	Traditional	PRA
20 – 30	12 (5.0)	14 (5.8)
30 – 40	52 (21.7)	69 (28.7)
40 – 50	59 (24.6)	14 (5.8)
50 and above	14 (5.8)	6 (2.5)
χ^2	29.252**	P < 0.01

(Figures in parentheses denotes per cent values)

A perusal of Table 5.30 reveals that age-group through PRA in animal husbandry activity has an impact. 28.7 per cent women respondents of 30-40 years age-group perform animal husbandry activity through PRA, whereas, 5.8 per cent women respondents of 20-30 years age-group does the same activity through PRA and 2.5 per cent women respondents of 50 and above age group perform in animal husbandry activity through PRA. The observed value of χ^2 (29.252**) was significant at 1 per cent level of significance.

Table 5.31. Impact of family type of farm women in dairy activity through PRA

Family type	Dairy activity	
	Traditional	PRA
Nuclear	89 (37.1)	93 (38.7)
Joint	48 (20.0)	10 (4.2)
χ^2	20.581**	P < 0.01

(Figures in parentheses denotes per cent values)

A perusal of Table 5.31 reveals family type impact through PRA in animal husbandry activity. Maximum (38.7%) women respondents of nuclear family system imparts animal husbandry activity through PRA whereas only 4.2 per cent women respondents of joint family system performed animal husbandry activity through PRA. The observed value of χ^2 (20.581**) was significant at 1 per cent level of significance.

Table 5.32. Impact of caste of farm women in dairy activity through PRA

Caste	Dairy activity	
	Traditional	PRA
Upper caste	17 (7.1)	30 (12.5)
OBC	88 (36.7)	47 (19.6)
SC/ST	32 (13.3)	26 (10.8)
χ^2	12.094*	P < 0.05

(Figures in parentheses denotes per cent values)

A perusal of Table 5.32 reveals that in caste-wise impact through PRA in animal husbandry activity, 19.6 per cent women respondents of OBC category involved in animal husbandry activity through PRA whereas 12.5 per cent upper caste women respondents were involved in animal husbandry activity through PRA. The observed value of χ^2 (12.094*) was significant at 5 per cent level of significance.

Table 5.33. Impact in dairy activity through education of farm women

Education	Dairy activity	
	Traditional	PRA
Illiterate	24 (10.0)	4 (1.7)
Primary	55 (22.9)	19 (7.9)
Secondary	30 (12.5)	18 (7.5)
High school	20 (8.3)	36 (15.0)
Intermediate & above	8 (3.3)	26 (10.8)
χ^2	44.986**	P < 0.01

(Figures in parentheses denotes per cent values)

It is revealed from Table 5.33 that in education-wise impact through PRA in dairy activity, 7.9 per cent women respondents educated up to primary level involved in animal husbandry activity through PRA whereas 1.7 per cent illiterate women respondents were involved herself in animal husbandry activity through PRA and 7.5 per cent women respondents were involved in animal husbandry activity through PRA and 7.5 per cent women respondents educated up to secondary level involved in animal husbandry activity through PRA. 15.0 per cent women respondents educated up to high school level were involved in animal husbandry activity through PRA. The observed value of χ^2 (44.986**) significant at 1 per cent level of significance.

Table 5.34. Impact of age group of farm women in household

Age-group (years)	Household activity	
	Traditional	PRA
20 – 30	18 (7.5)	8 (3.3)
30 – 40	61 (25.4)	60 (25.0)
40 – 50	55 (22.9)	18 (7.5)
50 and above	13 (5.4)	7 (2.9)
χ^2	12.911*	P < 0.05

(Figures in parentheses denotes per cent values)

A perusal of Table 5.34 reveals the impact of age group of farm women in household activity, 25.0 per cent women have belonged to 30 to 40 years age group doing household through PRA whereas, 7.5 per cent farm women have belonged to 40 to 50 years age group doing household activity impact of PRA. The observed value of χ^2 (12.911*) was significant at 5 per cent level of significance at 3 d.f. conclude that age group of farm women affected the impact of the PRA technique.

Table 5.35. Impact of education of farm women in household activity

Education	Household activity	
	Traditional	PRA
Illiterate	23 (9.6)	5 (2.1)
Primary	60 (25.0)	14 (5.8)
Secondary	18 (7.5)	30 (12.5)
High school	28 (11.7)	28 (11.7)
Intermediate & above	18 (7.5)	16 (6.7)
χ^2	32.794**	P < 0.01

(Figures in parentheses denotes per cent values)

Data presented in Table 5.35 reveals the impact of education of farm women in household activity through PRA technique. 12.5 per cent farm women were educated up to secondary level aware in household activity through PRA whereas, 11.7 per cent farm women educated up to high school standard using household activity through PRA technique. 6.7 per cent farm women respondents educated up to intermediate and above standard using household activity through PRA technique. The observed value of χ^2 (32.794**) significant at 1 per cent level of significance at 4 d.f. conclude that education of farm women effected the technique.

Table 5.36 shows the problems and prioritization faced by farm women either on a regular basis or at different times but it can be of different kinds and they reveal them if they

Table 5.36. Constraints faced by farm women in adoption of PRA technique

Problem	Yes	No	Scores	Rank
Social problems				
(a) Cruelty and repression	160 (66.7)	80 (33.3)	1.67	V
(b) Divorce by husband	114 (47.5)	126 (52.5)	1.47	X
(c) Re-marry	95 (39.6)	145 (60.4)	1.39	XII
(d) Dowry	215 (89.6)	25 (10.4)	1.89	I
(e) Wife beating	147 (61.2)	93 (38.8)	1.61	VII
(f) Large number of children	132 (55.0)	108 (45.0)	1.55	IX
Economic problems				
(a) Shortage of land	174 (72.5)	66 (27.5)	1.72	III
(b) Shortage of cash	204 (85.0)	36 (15.0)	1.85	II
Infrastructure problems				
(a) Drinking water	138 (57.5)	102 (42.5)	1.57	VIII
(b) Problem of latrine	68 (28.3)	172 (71.7)	1.28	XIV
(c) Problem of transport	152 (63.3)	88 (36.7)	1.63	VI
(d) Problem of medical treatment	168 (70.0)	72 (30.0)	1.70	IV
(e) Shortage of housing	88 (36.7)	152 (63.3)	1.37	XIII
Religious problem				
Harassment by fundamentalists	111 (46.2)	129 (53.8)	1.46	XI

(Figures in parentheses denotes per cent values)

find opportunities for doing so. It appears that giving dowry is the most serious problem and wife beating and having large number of children. The first problem (1.89%) directly reflects their socio-economic position as regards dowry which they find very difficult to provide while getting their daughters married. Wife beating causes both physical and mental repression while bearing of a large number of children (1.55) is a problem which they are unable to cope up with. The social problems within households and those relating to fundamentalists arise because the women feel repressed and are not in a position to assert their rights and privileges. It calls for economic and social empowerment of women whether on the basis of actions taken by state or other non-government development organizations. Groups of men and women in village communities or village level organizations can also play a significant role in diminishing the intensity of the stated problems. The economic problems of finding cash (1.85%) and owing land are related to poverty and can be resolved through appropriate packages of poverty reduction programmes. Religious problem harassment by fundamentalist (1.46%) were found in rural areas due to literacy. Rural women have their own stock of rural knowledge because of the nature of work they perform. Their busy schedule does not spare them much time and with whatever time they find they engage themselves in other income generating activities. Rural women are deprived and discriminated upon in several ways.

Table 5.37. Effect of approaches on PRA.

Approach	Frequency	Per cent
Groups	192	80.0
Mass	36	15.0
Individual	12	5.0
Total	**240**	**100.0**

The perusal of Table 5.37 reveals the per cent approaches affected the farm women. In PRA team there must be female scientists in the team so that rural women could be effectively involved in the appraisal exercise, while interacting with the villagers she should not jump directly to the objective of the study but first develop rapport with them listen to what they say, encourage them to join the discussion, review discussed and noted down, 80.0 per cent farm women were aware about PRA technique whose approaches in a group while 15.0 per cent farm women have found profitable technique in a mass.

Minimum 5.0 per cent farm women have gain PRA technique whose presence in individuals. The team members should make efforts to perform the activities that the villagers are doing such as sowing seeds, transplanting, harvesting, threshing, feeding, milking and chaffing.

Table 5.38. Participation of institution in PRA technique

Name of Institution	Overall per cent	Posticipation
Agricultural University	70.0	30.0
Agricultural government bodies	35.0	10.0
KVKs	50.0	22.0
NGOs	3.0	-
Extension workers	8.0	2.5
Progressive farmers	14.0	3.0

Table 5.38 indicates that 70.0 per cent agricultural universities, 35.0 per cent agricultural government bodies 50.0 per cent KVKs, 14.0 per cent progressive farmers, 8.0 per cent extension workers and 3.0 per cent NGOs were involved to train farm women through PRA technique. Hence 2.5 per cent farm women participate through extension workers and 3.0 per cent through progressive farmers. PRA is not mere casual application of field techniques at random but there is a much larger process involved preparation of mindsets for listening and learning inculcation of values, which support skills for learning rapidly improves with daily reflections and exercises in embracing errors. PRA techniques involves in such areas and understanding the physical ecological and socio-economic dimensions of the issues concerned. The importance of institutions was on the basis of their potential to be of use to the community. Having percentage involvement of the institutions explained the rationale for the ranking.

The interpretation of Table 5.39 reveals the correlation coefficient between variables and three household activities positively correlated with age, education, caste, income (0.4883*), family size (0.4062*) and land holding (0.4711*).

Agriculture activity are significantly correlated with income (0.4162*) and education (0.3617*). Dairy activity are positively significantly correlated with education (0.4907*), income (0.4918*), family size (0.3458*) and land holding (0.4517*). PRA is a way of organizing people for collecting and analyzing information within a short time span.

Table 5.39. Correlation coefficient between independent variables and agriculture and household activity

Variables	Correlation coefficient		
	Agriculture activity	Dairy activity	Household activity
Age	-0.3812	-0.1901	0.2818*
Education	0.3617*	0.4907*	0.4516*
Caste	0.1021	0.2399	0.3109*
Income	0.4162*	0.4918*	0.4883*
Family size	-0.1175	0.3458*	0.4062*
Land holding	0.1612	0.4517*	0.4711*

Constraints

Rural women face different problems either on a regular basis or at different times, many of which are not easy to resolve on account of societal perceptions and other factors. The problems can be of different kinds and they reveal them if they find opportunities for doing so. Given a chance, the rural women can describe their problems and prioritise them according to their perceptions.

Table 5.40 shows the constraints faced by farm women in various activities, patriarchial social factor (31.7%) faced by farm women in dairy activity and 24.2 per cent women in agriculture activity. 59.2 per cent farm women have faced purda system in household activity whereas, 42.5 per cent women in agriculture activity. 83.3 per cent women have faced illiteracy educational factor in household activity whereas, 32.9 per cent women in dairy activity. 41.2 per cent women were dropout due to educational factor in household problem

Table 5.40. Constraints of the farm women according to PRA activities during daily work

Constraints	Agriculture	Dairy	Household
Social factor			
(1) Patriarchial factor	58 (24.2)	76 (31.7)	22 (9.2)
(2) Purda system	102 (42.5)	86 (35.8)	142 (59.2)
Educational factor			
(1) Illiteracy	56 (23.3)	79 (32.9)	200 (83.3)
(2) High rate of dropout	48 (20.0)	52 (21.7)	99 (41.2)
Economic factor			
(1) Low status	88 (36.7)	67 (27.9)	168 (70.0)
(2) Lack of decision power	133 (55.4)	62 (25.8)	192 (80.0)
(3) No right in economic	188 (78.3)	51 (21.2)	96 (40.0)
Cultural factor			
(1) Caste system	94 (39.2)	64 (26.7)	108 (45.0)
(2) Gender discrimination	212 (88.3)	112 (46.7)	42 (17.5)
(3) Dominant group	162 (67.5)	81 (33.7)	40 (16.7)
(4) Open society	48 (20.0)	50 (20.8)	74 (30.8)
(5) Conservative and traditional society	72 (30.0)	41 (17.1)	92 (38.3)
Environmental factor			
(1) Less transportation	158 (65.8)	66 (27.5)	6 (2.5)
(2) Weather dependency	207 (86.2)	12 (5.0)	2 (0.8)
(3) High rate of pregnancy	6 (2.5)	19 (7.9)	173 (72.1)
(4) Work burden	89 (37.1)	27 (11.2)	158 (65.8)
(5) Malnutrition & ill health	26 (10.8)	63 (26.2)	136 (56.7)

(Figures in parentheses denotes per cent values)

whereas, 21.7 per cent in dairy activity. 70.0 per cent women respondents have low economic status in household activity whereas 36.7 per cent women in agriculture activity. 80.0 per

FINDINGS AND DISCUSSION 101

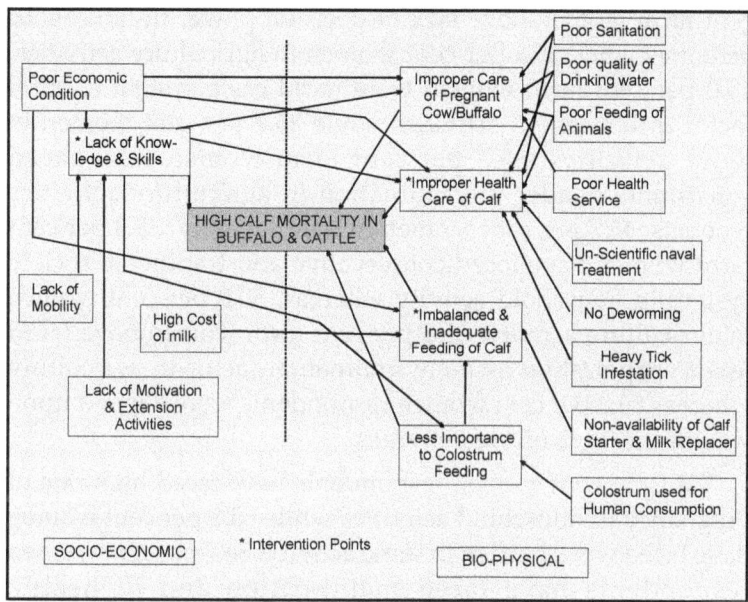

Fig. 5.12. Problem—Cause Diagram.

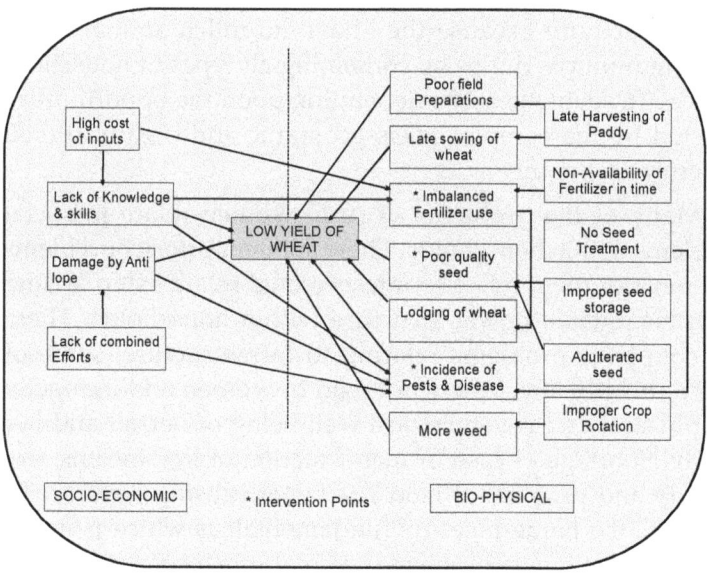

Fig. 5.13. Problem—Cause Diagram.

cent farm women have lack of decision power in household activities while 55.4 per cent women in agriculture activities. 45.0 per cent farm women were faced caste system cultural factor in household activities while 26.7 per cent women in dairy activities. 88.3 per cent farm women were faced constraints gender discrimination in agriculture activities whereas, 46.7 per cent women in dairy activity. 38.3 per cent farm women have faced conservative and traditional society system in household activity whereas, 30.0 per cent women in agriculture activity. 65.8 per cent farm women have faced less transportation as a environmental factor in agriculture whereas 86.2 per cent women respondents were depend upon weather in agriculture activities.

72.1 per cent women respondents have faced high rate of pregnancy in household activities while 65.8 per cent women have faced work burden in same activity. 56.7 per cent women respondents have faced malnutrition and ill health; environmental factor in household activity due to work load, more facility size and low status whereas 26.2 per cent women in dairy activity because they have no milch animal. They perform multiple duties by combining all types of household work with such other jobs depending upon the opportunities affected by the complex socio-economic and organizational structure of the life.

Many of the problems of rural women relate to social problems within households. These are their priority problems and most of them relate to interpersonal relationship arising from inequitable power structure within households. There are couple of problems relating to infrastructure, some of which directly affect the work-load of women and indirectly the physical and psychological well-being of herself and her family. Shortage of cash of manifestation of low income and poverty and problem of land is a factor causing poverty. To top it all, the harassment by fundamentalists which is in the nature of a religious problem is also of much consequence to the women who perceive it as a form of repression.

The social problems within households and those relating to fundamentalists arise because the women feel repressed and are not in a position to assert their rights and privileges. It calls for economic and social empowerment of women whether on the basis of action taken by state or other non-government development organizations. For motion of pressure groups of men and women in village communities or village level organizations can also play a significant role in diminishing the intensity of the stated problems. The other economic problems of finding cash and owning land are related to poverty and can be resolved through appropriate packages of poverty reduction programmes.

Chapter 6: Summary and Conclusion

In our society, where economic power rests with the men, convention decreed that women's place in the home, and that her husband's words care the law. They share the duties and responsibilities of maintaining their families in more than equal term with their men-folks but because of low visibility of their contribution, they are not regarded as equal partners in development process in spite of legal and constitutional equality. Women are the cultural victims in our society, which provides superiority to men and institutionalizes deprivation to women. Though, they play dual roles, but patriarchal farming system forced them behind four walls of the house.

PRA technique not only draw on the complexity and sophistication of people's technical and social knowledge and their practical expertise in managing livelihoods (etc.), but also draw on hitherto unrecognized abilities of diagrammatic and symbolic representation among informants through a range of mapping and other technique useable by non literate people.

Objectives

1. To study socio-economic status of farm women.
2. To study the involvement and time utilization of women in farm and home activities through PRA
3. Impact of participation of farm women in PRA technique.

4. Constraints faced by farm women in the adoption of PRA techniques during daily work.

5. To suggest suitable measures for enhancing the use of PRA techniques.

Research Methodology

The study was conducted in Kanpur district. Two blocks were selected namely Kalyanpur and Sarsaul. Two villages were selected from each block. Thus, total 10 villages were selected in this study area. 24 farm women were selected from each village. Thus, total sample size were selected to 240. Dependent and independent variables were used such as age, caste, education, PRA technique, constraints etc. The statistical tools were used such as 't' test, χ^2 test and weightage mean.

Major Findings

1. 50.4 per cent farm women belong to 30 to 40 years age group whereas 30.4 per cent women were in 40 to 50 years age group. 10.8 per cent women respondents were belong to 20 to 30 years age groups whereas 8.4 per cent women in 50 and above age group. It means that women when become middle aged they generally get involved in work be it agricultural activity.

2. 56.3 per cent women respondents were belong to OBC category whereas, 24.1 per cent women of SC/ST category. Only 19.6 per cent farm women belonged to upper caste. PRA techniques efficiently treated through relating them with different aspects of village life rather than treating them through direct probing. PRA sessions on different aspects of village life related to caste and religion.

3. 77.1 per cent farm women have 5 members family size whereas 22.9 per cent women have 6 and above members family size. For monitoring by PRA methods

there can be a set of indicators proposed indigenously to guide effective implementation of family size.

4. 32.9 per cent women have earned Rs. 1501 to Rs. 3000 monthly whereas 25.8 per cent farm women have earned Rs. 3001 to Rs. 4500 monthly. 18.7 per cent women respondents have earned Rs. 4501 to Rs. 6000 monthly whereas 15.9 per cent women earned up to Rs. 1500 monthly.

5. 65.0 per cent farm women were having family annual income up to Rs. 50,000 whereas 35.0 per cent women respondents have annual family income Rs. 50001 and above.

6. 40.0 per cent women possessed marginal land whereas 31.2 per cent farm women have no land for farming. 24.2 per cent women have small land while 4.6 per cent farm women have large land holding belonged to high economic status.

7. 69.2 per cent farm women were doing farming whereas 22.5 per cent farm women were labourers. 4.6 per cent women respondents were engaged in business whereas 2.9 per cent women were in service. Women were carrying out farming activity through PRA.

8. 72.5 per cent women were having mixed house whereas 20.0 per cent women have pucca house. Only 7.5 per cent women have Kaccha house.

9. 13.7 per cent large land holder women respondents have tractor whereas 7.5 per cent small land women respondents have tractor. 17.9 per cent women have thresher, 25.0 per cent tube well, 20.8 per cent winnower and 13.3 per cent women have bullocks they were large land holding respondents. In small land holding 19.2 per cent women have tube well, 4.6 per cent women have generator, 12.1 per cent women have bullocks and 15.0 per cent women have *Phawada* and *Khurpi*. 20.0 per cent women who were landless have *Khurpi* and *Phawada*.

10. 51.7 per cent farm women have buffaloes whereas 30.0 per cent farm women have cow for milk business 10.8 per cent farm women have goat while 7.5 per cent farm women have poultry. On the basis of above analysis it was concluded that the buffalo is the most common milch animal among farmers.

11. 80.0 per cent farm women were aware about PRA technique whose approaches in a group while 15.0 per cent farm women have found profitable technique in a mass. Minimum 5.0 per cent farm women have gain PRA technique whose presence was in individual. The team members should make efforts to perform the activities that the villagers are doing such as sowing seeds, transplanting, harvesting, threshing, feeding, milking and chaffing.

12. 70.0 per cent agricultural universities 35.0 per cent agricultural government bodies 50.0 per cent KVKs, 14.0 per cent progressive farmers, 8.0 per cent extension workers, 3.0 per cent NGOs were involved to train farm women through PRA technique. 2.5 per cent farm women participate through extension workers and 3.0 per cent through progressive farmers. PRA is not mere casual application of field techniques at random but there is a much larger process involved preparation of mindsets for listening and learning inculcation of values.

13. 14.0 per cent farm women were involved to make seasonal food calendar through PRA and 15.0 per cent farm women were involved in time line and seasonal analysis pest disease and crop respectively. 12.0 per cent farm women have used food protection benefits through PRA whereas 10.0 per cent women respondents have used land use map technique through PRA. Only 8.0 per cent farm women have used resource map through PRA technique in study area, map and history of land, crop and season.

14. 8.3 per cent time in seasonal food calendar, 6.3 per cent time in seasonal analysis pest diseases and crop, 6.3 per cent in land use map and resource map respectively. In *Kharif* season farm women spent 8.3 per cent in time line, 6.3 per cent time in seasonal food calendar, land use map and food protection benefits respectively. In *Zaid* season farm women spent her time 4.2 per cent in time line and 2.1 per cent time in other agricultural activities through PRA. Rural livelihoods are integrally connected with seasonality.

15. 65.0 per cent women were used traditional method in farm operation whereas 55.0 per cent women respondents used milk yield by traditionally. In case of manure like compost and gobar gas plant, mostly farm women have used through PRA technique. 45.0 per cent women respondents have used drafting through PRA technique. 65.0 per cent women respondents were used methods through PRA for sale purpose of dairy products.

16. Maximum time spent of farm women in milk yield. 8.3 per cent in winter and summer. Farm women spent her time 4.2 per cent time in meat production in winter and summer season. In compost and cow dung manure, farm women spent her time 6.2 per cent in winter and summer season while in rainy season she spent her less time in these activities. For drafting in all season and they spent her time in same manner, 6.2 per cent time in summer season for additional income by milk product. In all animal husbandry activities mostly worked out by women and minimum involvement of women in animal sale, making models and animal grazing.

17. 75.0 per cent farm women have used traditionally technique for sweeping and cleaning house whereas 70.0 per cent farm women were involved in traditionally cleaning utensils. 92.0 per cent farm women traditionally adopted method for fetching water for cooking and

70.0 per cent farm women were preparing food traditionally. Through PRA 35.0 per cent, 45.0 per cent farm women were making weaving mats and weaving fences from bamboo sticks. Community empowerment would enhance their level of involvement in the development process.

18. Landless women respondents spent her 6.2 per cent time in sweeping and cleaning house, 8.3 per cent time in cleaning utensils, 4.2 per cent time giving fodder to cattle and goats, fetching water for cooking and child rearing. Apart from work in agriculture activities, dairy activity the rural farm women also have a busy schedule of household work.

19. 50.8 per cent Farm women were involved in commercial crop whereas 30.0 per cent involved in floriculture and scoring reveal priorities and preferences. Rural farm women have integrally connected with season. Each season has its own problems and the farm women have different strategies for their livelihoods. The seasons bear heavily on the physical conditions which in turn influence their lives. Seasons bring about differences in climatic conditions, in crops grown, in availability of water, food, fuel and fodder which in turn influence the living conditions in rural areas. In dairy activity rural farm women have involved 80.0 per cent in selling cow dung compost and 75.0 per cent in selling milk, whereas 30.0 per cent farm women were involved in selling milk product. Rural women were reluctant to participate for many reasons.

20. Farm women spent 7 hrs in April in agriculture activity, 7.5 hrs in May. 6.0 hrs in June, 5.0 hrs in July, 6.0 hrs in August and 7.0 hrs in March. Thus in harvesting and sowing time of crop in *Rabi* and *Kharif* season farm women spent her maximum time. In rainy season like July and August farm women have spent her less time in dairy activity because they were not making cow

dung cake, manure and grazing animals. Farm women spent her 2 hrs per day in dairy activity in the month of December, January, February and March. In household activities farm women spent her time average 6.0 hrs per day in various practices cleaning, washing, preparing food and child rearing. Farm women found time from agriculture activity she spent that in household activity.

21. Farm women spend different hours per day in activities like feeding children, cooking, fetching water, grazing livestock, collecting firewood and fuel wood. It is possible to identify general patterns from daily patterns. Daily routines can also be depicted on a seasonal basis in order to identify constraints and workloads of different groups related to different activities. Landless women have given maximum time to farming while marginal land owner women have given in farming and home activities. Small land and large land owner women spend time in home and time for self. Landless farm women were generally expend more her time in income generating household activities and 12.5 per cent time in work home. Marginal land holding farm women were spent her time (16.7 %) in income generating household activities while small land holding farm women were spent her time (16.7 %) in work home like fetching water, preparing food, feeding child and cleaning utensils. Large land holding farm women respondents have spent her time (20.8 %) in home work and 8.3 per cent time in income generating activity and time for self respectively.

22. Estimates of return from production to compare traditional and PRA, Rs. 200/ha in paddy, Rs. 50/ha in wheat, Rs. 125/ha in maize, Rs. 75/ha in jowar and Rs. 250/ha in *Sarson*. Most farm women were not proper literate and some were illiterate, they arrived at estimates of earnings from crops grown, dairy activities and household activities. In dairy return the PRA techniques are more useful than traditional in milk

selling which increases the milk production and selling of milk products. Depletion and degradation of forests are those of indigenous activities to which farm women have an integral relationship and bear the brunt with its rapid degradation and disappearance.

23. 32.1 per cent women respondents belong to OBC category involved in agricultural activity through PRA whereas 8.3 per cent SC/ST women respondents were involved in agricultural activity through PRA.

24. Maximum (37.9%) women respondents belong to nuclear family system involved in agriculture activity through PRA whereas, 14.2 per cent rural respondents were belong to joint family system involved in agriculture activity through PRA.

25. 14.2 per cent women respondents educated up to primary level involved in agriculture activity through PRA whereas 2.5 per cent illiterate women respondents involve herself in agriculture activity through PRA. 10.0 per cent women respondents educated up to secondary level were involved in agriculture activity through PRA and 15.0 per cent women respondents educated up to high school level were involved in agriculture activity through PRA.

26. 14.6, 9.6 and 2.9 per cent women respondents having small land holding, landless and large land holding respectively, imparts agricultural activities through PRA.

27. 28.7 per cent women respondents of 30-40 years age-group perform animal husbandry activity through PRA, whereas, 5.8 per cent women respondents of 20-30 years age-group does the same activity through PRA and 2.5 per cent women respondents of 50 and above age group perform in animal husbandry activity through PRA.

28. Maximum (38.7%) women respondents of nuclear family system imparts animal husbandry activity through PRA whereas only 4.2 per cent women respondents of joint

family system performed animal husbandry activity through PRA.

29. 19.6 per cent women respondents of OBC category involved in animal husbandry activity through PRA whereas 12.5 per cent upper caste women respondents were involved in animal husbandry activity through PRA.

30. 7.9 per cent women respondents educated up to primary level involved in animal husbandry activity through PRA whereas 1.7 per cent illiterate women respondents were involved herself in animal husbandry activity through PRA and 7.5 per cent women respondents were involved in animal husbandry activity through PRA and 7.5 per cent women respondents educated up to secondary level involved in animal husbandry activity through PRA. 15.0 per cent women respondents educated up to high school level were involved in animal husbandry activity through PRA.

31. 12.5 per cent farm women were educated up to secondary level aware in household activity through PRA whereas, 11.7 per cent farm women educated up to high school standard using household activity through PRA technique. 6.7 per cent farm women respondents educated up to intermediate and above standard using household activity through PRA technique.

32. Dowry problem (1.89 %) directly reflects their socio-economic position which they find very difficult to provide while getting their daughters married. Wife beating causes both physical and mental repression while bearing of a large number of children (1.55) is a problem which they are unable to cope up with. The social problems within households and those relating to fundamentalists arise because the women feel repressed and are not in a position to assert their rights and privileges. It calls for economic and social

empowerment of women whether on the basis of actions taken by state or other non government development organizations.

33. The economic problems of finding cash (1.85 %) and owing land are related to poverty and can be resolved through appropriate packages of poverty reduction programmes. Religious problem harassment by fundamentalist (1.46 %) was found in rural areas due to literacy.

34. Patriarchal social factor (31.7 %) faced by farm women in dairy activity and 24.2 per cent women in agriculture activity. 59.2 per cent farm women have faced purda system in household activity whereas, 42.5 per cent women in agriculture activity. 83.3 per cent women have faced illiteracy educational factor in household activity whereas, 32.9 per cent women in dairy activity. 41.2 per cent women were dropout due to educational factor in household problem whereas, 21.7 per cent in dairy activity. 70.0 per cent women respondents have low economic status in household activity whereas, 36.7 per cent women in agriculture activity. 80.0 per cent farm women have lack of decision power in household activities while 55.4 per cent women in agriculture activities. 45.0 per cent farm women were faced caste system cultural factor in household activities while 26.7 per cent women in dairy activities.

Suggestions and Policy Implication

1. Income based classification of household would logically recommend increase in income through income generation scheme.

2. Each village community has its own resource endowment, natural resource base, socio-economic features, problems, priorities and preferences.

3. The villagers can organize themselves for community action. Community involvement builds upon

sustainable use of local resources and strengthens community self reliance.

4. Community empowered can play a powerful role in creating a sustainable system of agriculture by use of local resources, lower dependence on external inputs and adopt agro-ecological technologies which are environment friendly.

5. A PRA can be conducted in such a manner that it raises expectations of positive things to happen, if expectations are unnecessarily raised and not followed up in due course the situation can turn to be problematic.

6. PRA is powerful methodology for rural development and it is important that its limitation are recognized and understood so as to use PRA for bringing about maximum benefit to the society.

7. Data generated through PRA can be for a person, household, village on group of villages.

8. The use of statistical tools in PRA data depends on the kind of data available statistical tools based on averages may not always be relevant for data analysis especially when the information generated through PRA is of a qualitative nature.

9. PRA as a methodology is not without its limits. Some of it limitations like changing of attitudes, problem of rapidly, cultural context of diagramming, problems in conducting PRA, raising people's expectations, sensitivity of issues, lack of enthusiasm etc. can phase as problem in its use.

10. Flexibility in use of participatory methods makes it possible for flexibility in probing of issues.

11. Through participatory methods qualitative attributes of natural resources and their importance can be highlighted by local users even when many of them cannot be quantified in numerical terms.

12. Visual methods of participation helps in visual representation where many can participate together in appraising natural resources.
13. Sequencing of participatory methods lead from one aspect of a topic to another for better understanding and discussion.
14. Participatory methods enable individual community members to participate as a group.
15. Women should be given a share in the property with institutional mechanisms developed to check fragmentation.
16. Women need to be involved with developmental programmes. More women extension functionaries may be employed in agriculture and allied departments to facilitate easy interaction and skill transfer.
17. Programmes for training and knowledge transfer should be tailor made for women. They need to be trained in soil sampling, composting, green manuring, germination tests and plant protection measures, eco-friendly farming, use of bio-fertilizers and bio-fertilizers and bio-pesticides, vermin-composting etc. Other areas include seed production, pest control, post harvest handling, processing, marketing etc.
18. Staff of development departments should be trained in PRA techniques to help them to understand the socio-cultural and economic conditions of women.
19. Researchers should develop an appreciation for the wealth of indigenous knowledge available with the farming communities. Farmer participatory approach, participatory planning of extension strategy for crop production programmes need to be adopted and followed.
20. Research institutions should focus research studies on problems of relevance for farm women. Priority should be given in developing low cost agricultural implements

for specific agricultural operations in which women participate to a large extent.

21. Women should be sensitized to their rights, opportunities, services and programmes. Media should play a critical role to sensitize the community to women related issues.

22. Training to farm women should be participatory. A few trained women should be selected and helped to practice technology with input supply on credit basis. These fields can be used as demonstration plots for training other women.

Bibliography

A time use study of Agricultural Farming by Women in Bangladesh (1998). Women's Involvement in Agricultural Farm Activities in Bangladesh. www.Sciencelinko-jp/j-east/article/200002-10k.

A.K. Mishra and K.V. Subrahmanyam (2004). Improving the Livelihood of Landless and Marginal Farmers Through. www.cipav.org.co/irrd18/5/mis2 18073.htm-131k.

Adewumi Olaniyi Matthuw (2007). This paper examines the constraints faced by SMSMME. www.aaae-africa.org/ghana.

Arjun, K. Sengupta (2005). Constraints Faced by Establishments. Homeworkers as a special category.

Azad India Foundation (2006). Women Employment in India—Employment Opportunity for Women...azadindia.org/Social-issues/women-Employment.html.

Azad Jammu and Kashmir (Wednesday, 25 May 2005) PRA techniques are the most suitable methodology which was used to conduct ... *www.ajk.gov.pk/site/index.*

Canegrowers Strategy for Women and Teams (2006). Women and leaders within the industry—ideas for enhancing women's participation in on farm activities leading to greater involvement. www.canegrowers.com/docs/ women Research-Sept. 06.

CIDA China Programme (2008) Taking an Anecdote and Generalizing. www.acdi-cida.go.ca/CIDAWEB/acdieida.ns.

Countdown Newsletter(2005)Header ... Participatory Wealth Ranking (PWR) is a modification of the Participatory Rural Appraisal (PRA) technique. *www.microcreditsummit.org/newsletter.*

Development of Sustainable Agriculture in the Pacific (Issue 16 - Aug – Sep 2005). Bi-Monthly Update -First PRA for DSAP French Polynesia...

- Extension officers train in PRA techniques... www.spc.int/ dsap/ newsletters_dsap_01.
Door E. Revath (2004). In the pre suicide situation most women used to work in the farm as wage labour or ... www.dehelling net.
Eko Nugraho, S.Pt.(2008). Fact of animal husbandry ...... about the role of philanthropy in women empowerment conducted by PRA. www.prasety. brawiojaya-ac.id.
FAO Corporate Document Repository (2004). Rural Women and Food Security in Asia and the Pacific. www.fao.org/docrep.
Gender and Development Plan of Action (2008). Men and especially women's involvement in forest activities and commercialization along with increased migration and off-farm activities are ..... ftp// ftp.fao.org/unfao/ bodies/conf/doc.
Halmes Tim (2001). A participatory approach in practice understanding field worker' use of PRA in Action Aid the Gambia' IDS Working paper 123. www.macp-pk.org/DOCS.
Hills Borough County Farm (2007). The Voice of Agriculture in, farm bureau and other organizations ..... www.hcfarmbureau-org/ programs.html.
Hindu Kush – Himalaya (2004). Around 750 men and women who are members of CTPL ..... The consteunts faced by different actors in the supply chains of the selected. www.mountainpartnership.org/mpp/ doc.
Impact Evaluation—Participatory Rural Appraisal (PRA) Techniques. The PRA facilitators introduce the technique using local terms for wealth and .... And how they would describe a poor household or a rich household (that is ..... web.worldbank org/WBSITE/.EXTERNAL/ TOPICS/ EXTPOVERTY/EXTISPOMA/O,,contentMDK:20190393-isCURL:Y-menuPK:41513...-44k.
Improve Integrated Dairy Production (2007). PRA technique was derived .... Likely to play a role in management of the activities on the farm. www. Springerlink-com/index/w010408551160831.
Improving the Effectiveness of Collective Action (July 2006) Community Forestry and Women Participation were reviewed and methodology by drawing on PRA technique www.capri.cgiar.org/CAPRIW54.
Interactive Multimedia Compact Disc (2007). It is the need of the hour to empower farm women in technology..... www.14donlione.net/ articles/ current-article.asp?
International Development Research Centre (2007). PRA technique facilitated and enabled the participation of men, women, girls. www.indre.ca/en/ev-28707-201-1Do-TOPIC.html.

Jadabamanda (2007). The New Millennium Women Entrepreneur Feb. 2007... The main objective of the Scheme is to Empowr women through development of their entrepreneurial skills ...... www.indianmber.com/ Faculty-column.

Jamal, Shagufta and Arya, H.P.J. (2004). Participatory Rural Appraisal in Agriculture and Animal Husbandry. A Training Manual pp. 1-2.

Jerome Destombes (2004). ASAVK Biannual Conference They have to secure extra domestic labour in order to farm without having. www.devstrud.org. uk/conference.

John R. Campbell (2001). Anthropology and Field Research on Farming Systems ... Most importantly, the role of the facilitator. www.resonfarm.org.

Jones Emma and Speech, (2001) "Of Other Spaces" situating participatory practices : a study from South India : IDS working paper 137.

Kiranjot Sindu (2007). A more of involvement of women in zone 2 in this otherwise male centered activity as compared to ... pation of women in farm activities. www.Krepublishers.com/HCS-01-1-0450-7-018.Sindu.

Kunwar, Neelma (2000). Community Mobilization for Self Help Group Formation, pp. 8-10.

Kunwar Neelma & Vashishtha, Priya (2003). A Practical Manual on Advances in Home Science Extension, pp. 16-17.

Kunwar, Neelma and Vashistha' Priya (2004). A Text Book of PRA and Methods for Community Participation, p. 1-1, 120-121.

Lauren Starr (2003). Western's Caucus on Women's Issues. Considering all the abstracts and difficulties that women faced. www.awo.ca/wcwi.

Lo Okitai, H.O. Ondwasy and M.P. Obali (1998). Gender issues in poultry production in rural households of Western—participatory Rural Appraisal techniques were used to collect. www.cipav.org.co/irrd.19/2/okit19017. htm-42k.

Mukerjee, Neela (2002). Participatory Learning and Action (with 100 field Methods). pp. 1-2.

Muthengi ki manzi, Speight Melanie & kilao Christine (2001) 'world Neighbours' Experience of going beyond Pra in Kenya' IDS working paper 132.

National Strategy Plan (2007). There is a lack of representation of farm women in off farm activities both ..... their involvement in decision making structures should also be supported. www.nwci.ic/content/download/267/ 1201/file/ruraldevstrat.06.doc.

Participation Pattern of Farm Women in Post Harvesting. A more of involvement of women in zone 2 in this. Otherwise male centered activity as compared to ..... pation of women in farm activities. Indian Journal ... www.krepublishers.com/.../HCS-01-1-045-07-018-Sidhu-K/HCS-01-1-045-07-018-Sidhu-K-Tt.pdf.

Participatory Mapping (2007). PRA introduce the technique using local terms for wealth. www.worldbank.org/

Pratt, Garet (2001). Practitioners critical reflections on PRA and participation in hepul IDS Worth paper, 122, www.macp-pk.org/DOCS.

Rabert Chambus (2006). Participation Resource Centre Notes for Participants in PRA a household history and profile, a farm ..... This applies even more strongly to women then to men. PRA methods often take ..... www.ides.ac.uk/ids/particip/research/pra/pres.

Raphael Abvodun Olawepo (2007). Using participatory rural appraisal to explore coastal fishing in ..... presence of other economic activities in the area. 4 methods of study and analysis. www.springerlink.com/index/41943817020QW8

Report Livelihood Assessment and Microfinance Programme (2004-05). It was observed during the PRA that about 300 women in Sandhakuda. www.orissafisheries.com/file/Reprot%20 on % 20 micro % 20 finance/doc.

Research Report Evaluation of Community Participation (2005) entailing PRA techniques such as Focused Group Discussions (FGDs) and Key If women, how do they get involved? (a) Planting trees around water sources. *www.unesco.org/mab/bursaries/mysrept/2005.*

Robert Chambers (2006) Participation Resource Centre Notes for Participants in PRA a household history and profile, a farm, ... This applies even more strongly to women than to men. PRA methods often take ... *www. ids.ac.uk/ids/particip/research/pra/pra.*

Rural Cooperatives (2007). More women's involvement resulting from jobs well done Rural...... www.find.articles-com/P/articles/mi-moKFU/doc.

Science Links Japan Women's Involvement in Agricultural Farm ..... Women's involvement in Agricultural Farm Activities in Bangladesh. A Time Use Study of Agricultural Farming of Women in Bangladesh.... Sciencelinks. jp /lj-east/article/200002/000020000299A1035213.php-10k.

Singh Kamal, (2001) 'Handing Over the Stick : The Global Spread of Participatory Approaches to Development. www.ids.ac.uk/ids/partic/index.

Tango International. The objective of the training was to provide staff with the necessary knowledge and skills to implement PRA tools and techniques in determining community....
www.tangointernational.com/index.php? Mh=48.mi=6-15k.

Thelma Paris (2004). Impact of migration and/or off-farm employment on roles of women ...... www.aciar.gov.av/project/PLIA.

Thelma Paris (2004). Impact of migration and/or off-farm employment on roles of women ......(2004) www.aciar.gov.av/project/PLIA.

Using Participatory Rural Appraisal to explore coastal fishing in ... presence of other economic activities in the area. 4 Methods of study and analysis. Data collection methods for this research relied on PRA techniques....
www.springerlink.com/index/4M4381770QW8R67W.pdf.

West Bank/Gaza (2004). To provide staff with the necessary knowledge and skills to implement PRA tools and techniques in determining community. www.tangointernational.com/index.php-15.k.

Workshop ISTECS Taw (2008). Fact of Animal Husbandry ...... about the Role of Philanthropy in Women Empowerment conducted by PRA-3. www.prasety.brawiojaya-ac.id/en.

Index

A

Action Aid in Bangalore, 2
Action Aid the Gambia (AATG), 19
Aga Khan Rural Support Programme (AKRSP), 2
Agrahyan, 68
Akbarpur, 34
AKRSP, 9
  in Ahmedabad, 2
All India Coordinated Research Project on Home Science, 28
Animal husbandry activity, 93
Aswin, 68
Auraiya and Bidhuna tahsils, 34
Azad India Foundation (2006), 26

B

Badagry area of Lagos State, 27
Baisakh, 68
Banstaol, 77
Bheetargaon, 38
Bhognipur, 34

C

Canada, 21
CARE, 22
Central Statistical Organization, 34
Chaitra, 68
Constraints faced by farm women, 12
Coordinated Research Project, 30

D

Depletion and degradation of forests, 90, 111
Diagnostic Surveillance Studies (DSS), 30

E

Economic Opportunity Surveys (EOS), 30
Economic status, 45, 106
Education, 45

F

FAO, 31, 32
Farming System Research (RSR), 29
Findings and discussion, 50-103
  constraints, 99-103
  involvement of farm women in agriculture activity through PRA technique time line, 63-76
  involvement of women in household activities through PRA technique, 77-79
  socio-economic status of farm women, 50-63
  time, 80-99
Findings, 105
Focus Group Discussion (FGD), 31

G

Gangapur, 38
Ghatampur, 34, 38
Globalization, 27

H

Hardoi, 33
Hillsborough County Farm Bureau Women Committee, 29
Hindu Kush Himalayas, 24
Household Livelihood Security, 22
How participatory is PRA, 7

I

Improve Integrated Dairy Production (21 Sept., 2007), 29
International Centre for Integrated Mountain Development (ICIMOD), 24
International Development Research Centre (2007), 29
International Institute for Environment and Development, 2
Introduction, 1-15
Ishwariganj, 38

J

Justification of the study, 14
Jyaistha, 68

K

Kalyanpur, 38
Kanpur tahsil, 38
Kanpur, 34
Kenya, 2
Kharif, 66, 108
Khurpi, 63, 106
Kohna, Kanhpur, 33
Kondangmerak Village (Malang Regency), 30
KRIBP, 7
Krishi Gram Vigyan Kendra in Ranchi, 2, 98, 107

L

Land holding, 98

M

Magh, 68
Material possession, 46
Media, 116
Mitchell, 8
MYRADA, 2, 9

N

National Environment Secretariat, 2
National Strategy Plan (NSP) 2007-2013, 26
National Women Council of Ireland, 26
NGO World Neighbours, 18
NGOs, 2, 5, 98, 107

O

OBC, 105
Objectives, 14, 104
Occupation, 45
Occupied Palestinian Territories, 22

P

Packages of poverty reduction programmes, 103, 113
Panchayat Ghar, 69
Pandu, 35
Participatory methods, 9
Participatory Rural Appraisal (PRA), 1, 2, 5, 15, 21, 27, 46, 55, 90, 107
Patara, 38
Phalgun, 68

Phawada, 63, 106
Physical and mental repression, 96
Poush, 68
PRA and rapport building, 6
Prempur, 38
Priortisation of problems of rural women, 13
Profile of the study area, 33-38
   area, 34
   distribution between urban and rural area, 38
   district Kanpur, 33
   location, 33-34
   population, 34
   river system and water resources, 35-38
      climate, 36
      Ganga, 35
      humidity, 37-38
      lakes, 36
      rainfall, 36-37
      rivers, 35
      temperature, 37
      Yamuna, 35-36
   sub-divisions tahsils, 34
   topography, 34-35

R

Rabert Chambers (2006), 27
Rabi, 66, 108
Ranupane and Banurejo, 30
Rapid Rural Appraisal (RRA), 9
Religious problem, 113
Research methodology, 39-49, 105
   district under study, 39-41
   hypotheses, 47
   locale of the study, 39
   selection of blocks, 41
   selection of respondents, 41
   statistical measurement, 47-49
   time of investigation, 47
   variables and their operationalization, 41
   variables and their operationalization: dependent variables, 46-47
   variables and their operationalization: independent variables, 41-46
   villages identifies for the study, 41
Review of literature, 16-32
   Adewumi, 24
   Arjun, 26
   Campbell, John R., 20
   Canegrowers' strategy for women and teams, 26
   CIDA China Programme, 31
   Destombes, Jerome, 22
   Door, E. Revath, 25
   FAO Corporate Document Repository, 24
   Garett, Pratt, 18
   gender and development plan of action, 31
   Hindu Kush-Himalaya, 24
   Holland, 16
   Holmes, 19
   IAAS World Congress in Belarus, 30
   interactive multimedia compact disc (IMCD), 28
   Jamal, 22
   Jone, 19
   Kimanzi, 18
   Mukherjee, 21

Muthengi, 20
Neelma, Kunwar, 18, 21
Obali, M.P., 17
Ondwasy, H.O., 17
Panda, Jadabaranda, 30
Paris, Thelma, 23
participatory rural appriasal (PRA) techniques participatory mapping, 27-28
report livelihood assessment and microfinance programme, 25
rural cooperatives, 30
Sidhu, Kiranjot, 28
Singh, 19
Starr, Lauren, 21
Subrahmanyam, K.V., 22
West Bank/Gaza, 22
workshop ISTECS, 31
Rind and Sengar, 35
River Ganga, 33, 35
River system and water resources, 35-38
River Yamuna, 35-36
Robert Chambers, 18
Robertson, 8

S

Salaha Samithi (farmers advisory committee), 22
Sarson, 110
Sawan, 68
SC/ST, 53, 105, 111
SEWA, 9
Singh, Hindu, 33
Soft Systems Analysis and Cognitive Mapping, 9
Soil conditions, 66
Some observations on women's problems, 13
SPEECH in Madurai, 2
Strengths of PRA, 4
Suggestions and policy implications, 113
Sustainable Agricultural Development, 31

T

TANGO, 22
Technology, 47
Transfer of Technology (ToT), 28

U

Unnao, 33
USA, 2
Utilization, 47

V

Vidhunu, 38
Village Concept Project, 30
Villages selected, 38

W

Water management, 66
Women and formal PRAs, 10

Y

Yamuna, 33

Z

Zaid, 66, 108